Smithville Ontario in Colour Photos, Saving Our History One Photo at a Time

Photography
by Barbara Raué
2018

Series Name:
Cruising Ontario

Book 194: Smithville

Cover photo: 235 Canborough Street, Page 46

Series Name: Cruising Ontario
Saving Our History One Photo at a Time
in colour photos

Books Available in Alphabetical Order:

Aberfoyle, Acton, Alton, Amherstburg, Ancaster, Arthur, Aylmer, Ayr, Belleville, Bloomingdale, Brantford, Brockville, Burford, Burlington, Caledon, Caledonia, Cambridge, Clifford, Conestogo, Delhi, Dorchester to Aylmer, Drayton, Drumbo, Dundas, Eden Mills, Elmira, Elora, Erin, Essex, Fergus, Goderich, Guelph, Hagersville, Hamilton, Hanover, Harriston, Hespeler, Jarvis, Kingston, Kingsville, Kitchener, Lake Superior, Linwood, Listowel, London, Lucknow, Merrickville, Mono, Mount Forest, Neustadt, New Hamburg, Newboro, Niagara-on-the-Lake, Oakville, Orangeville, Orillia, Owen Sound, Palmerston, Paris, Perth, Peterborough, Petrolia, Port Colborne, Port Elgin, Portland, Preston, Rockwood, Sarnia, Sault Ste. Marie, Seaforth, Sheffield, Shelburne, Simcoe, Smiths Falls, Southampton, St. George, St. Jacobs, St. Marys, St. Thomas, Stoney Creek, Stratford, Thamesford, Thunder Bay, Tillsonburg, Waterdown, Waterford, Waterloo, Welland, Wellesley, Westport, Windsor, Wingham, Woodstock

Book 184: Mt Pleasant, Onondaga, Newport
Book 185-186: Grimsby
Book 187: Toronto
Book 188: Collingwood
Book 189-193: St. Catharines
Book 194: Smithville

Other Books by Barbara Raue

Coins of Gold

Arrows, Indians and Love

The Life and Times of Barbara
Volume 1: Inventions That Have Enhanced My Life
Volume 2: Entertainment That I Have Enjoyed
Volume 3: East Coast Trips
Volume 4: Olympics Have Always Intrigued Me
Volume 5: Wonders of the World
Volume 6: Caribbean Cruises We Have Enjoyed
Volume 7: Animals
Volume 8: Storms and Other Major Disasters in My Lifetime
Volume 9: Wars, Terrorist Attacks and Major Disasters

The Cromwell Family Book

Laura Secord Discovered

Daddy Where Are You?

Montana Series
Book 1: Montana Dream
Book 2: Life on the Montana Frontier
Book 3: Montana to Boston and Back
Book 4: Montana Sons Go to War
Book 5: Montana Sons Return From War

Visit Barbara's website to view all of her books
http://barbararaue.ca

Table of Contents

Station Street   Page 6

West Street   Page 15

Griffin Street   Page 22

St. Catharine Street   Page 29

Canborough Street   Page 39

Architectural Terms   Page 52

Building Styles   Page 57

West Lincoln is a township in the Niagara Region of Ontario. Main urban areas are located along provincial Highway 20. The administrative center of West Lincoln is the community of Smithville, situated between Hamilton and Niagara Falls.

Smithville was first settled by Richard Griffin and his family, United Empire Loyalists who came from Nine Partners, New York in 1787. The names of his sons were Abraham, Edward, Nathaniel, Isaiah, Smith, Jonathan, and Richard Jr. They settled on the Twenty Mile Creek in Grimsby (later South Grimsby) Township. Solomon Hill, who married Bethia, daughter of Richard Griffin, settled on Lot 6, Charles Meredith on Lot 7; Thomas Harris on Lot 11, and Thomas North on Lot 12. These lots, all in the 9th Concession became the settlement first known as Griffintown, but later renamed after Mrs. Griffin, whose maiden name was Mary Smith.

Edward "Ned" Griffin is sometimes claimed to be the real founder of the village. He was the one who felled the first tree, chose the village site, cleared the first acre of land, built the first house, and lived his entire life in the village. Another son, Smith Griffin, is credited with building a treadwheel in 1810. Settlers who wanted their grain ground were required to provide their own motive power by putting their oxen on the tread. Later, Smith Griffin built a dam and mill on the Twenty Mile Creek, making the treadmill obsolete. Smith also started an ashery, while his brother Edward opened a general store.

By 1849, Smithville had reached a population of about 150, and had been granted a post office with twice-weekly delivery. The settlement had a grist mill, a saw mill, a carding machine and cloth factory, four stores, one machine shop, one tannery, two blacksmiths, two tailors and two shoemakers.

Smithville, along with the remainder of South Grimsby Township was amalgamated into the newly formed Township of West Lincoln on January 1, 1970.

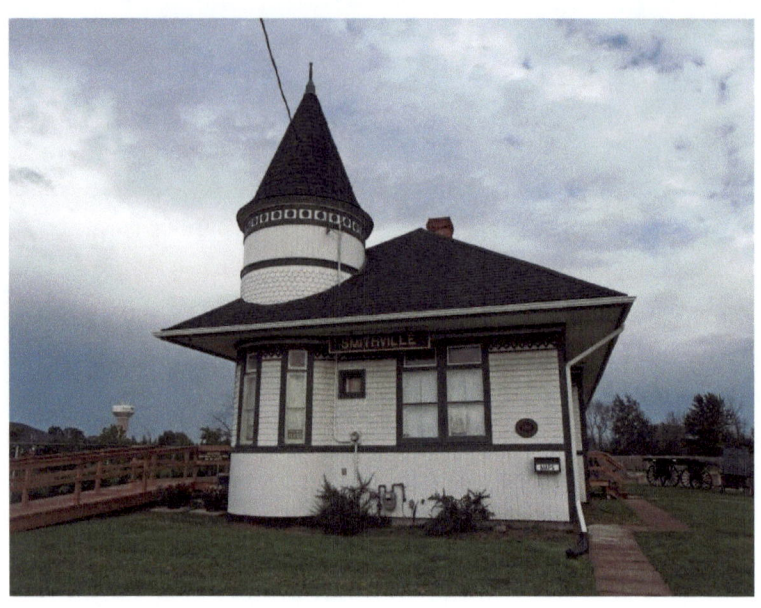

228 Station Street – Smithville Train Station established 1903 – hipped roof with turret

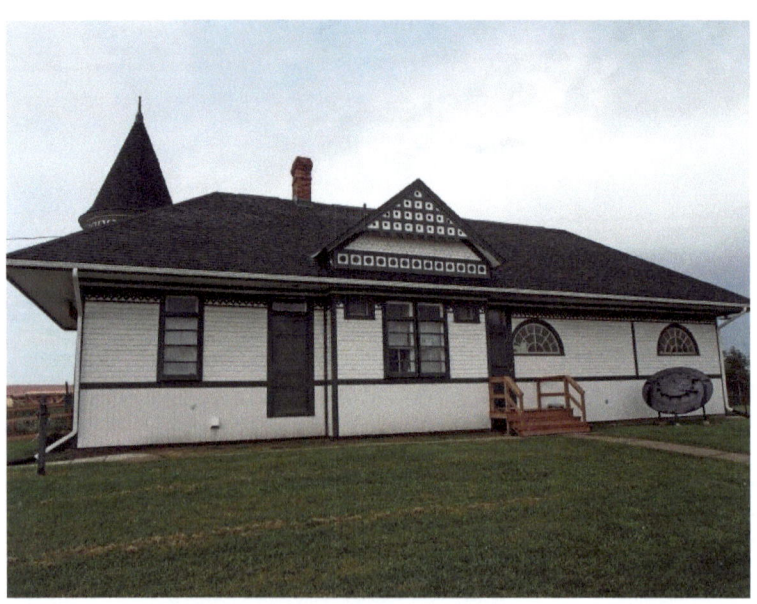

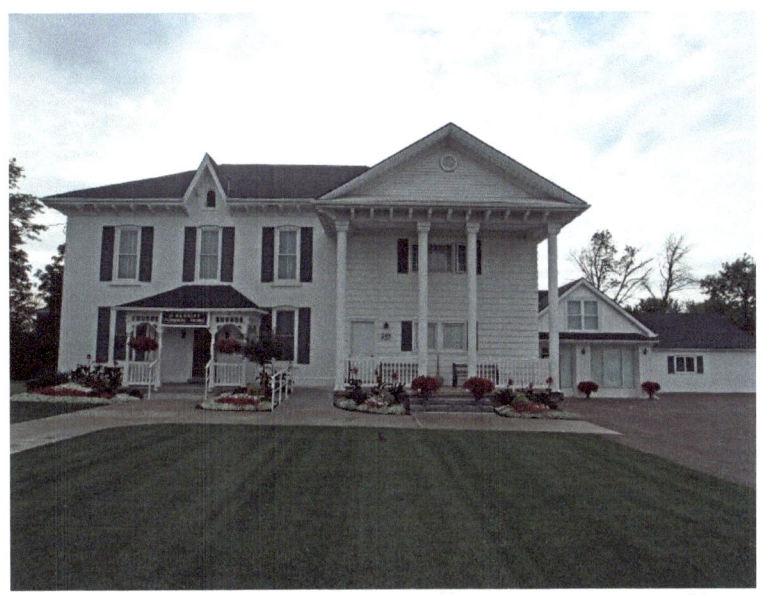

287 Station Street – two storey pillars support a pediment

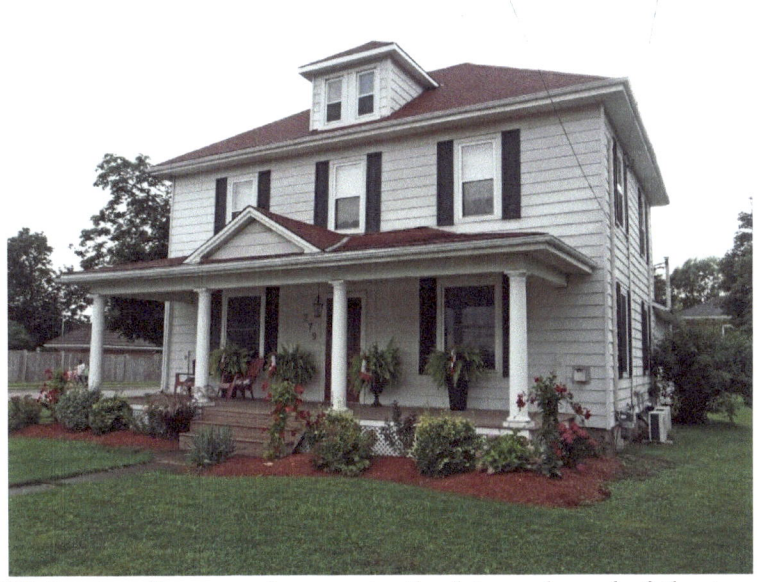

279 Station Street – dormer in the hipped roof of the two-storey home, Doric pillars supporting a veranda roof with a pediment

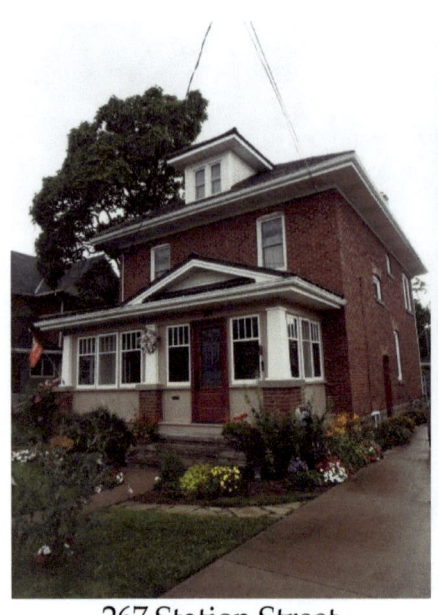
267 Station Street
Hipped roof, dormer, pediment

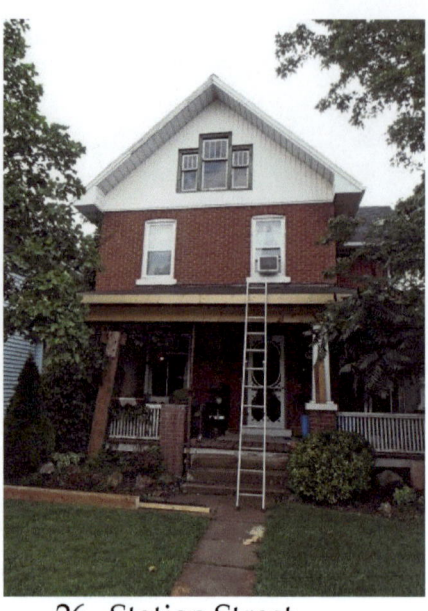
26_ Station Street
Palladian window in gable

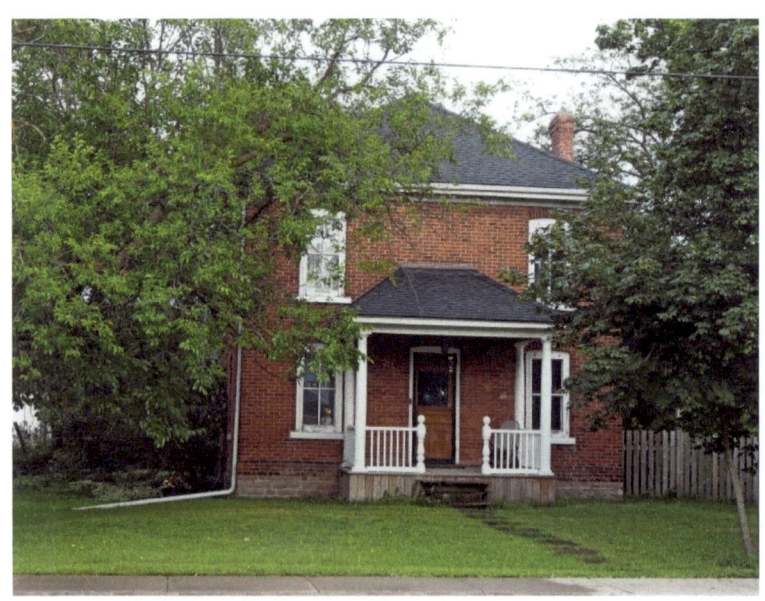
254 Station Street – hipped roof

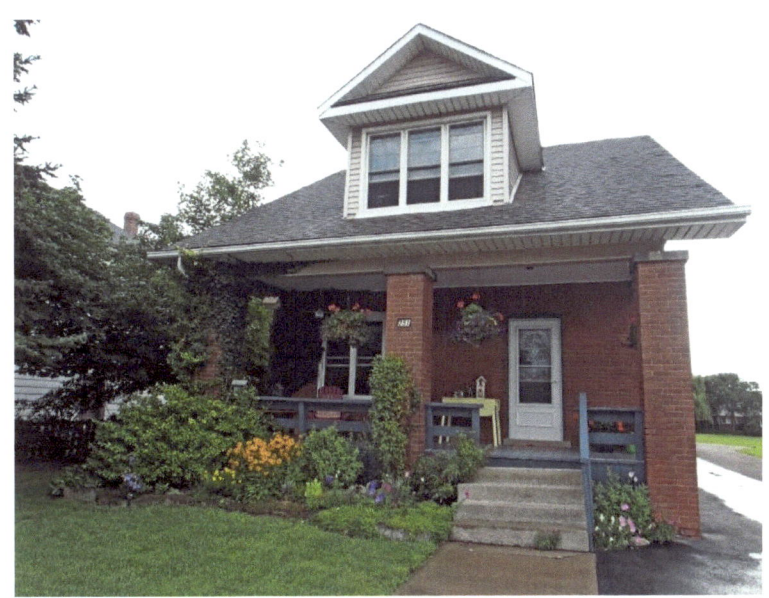

251 Station Street - dormer

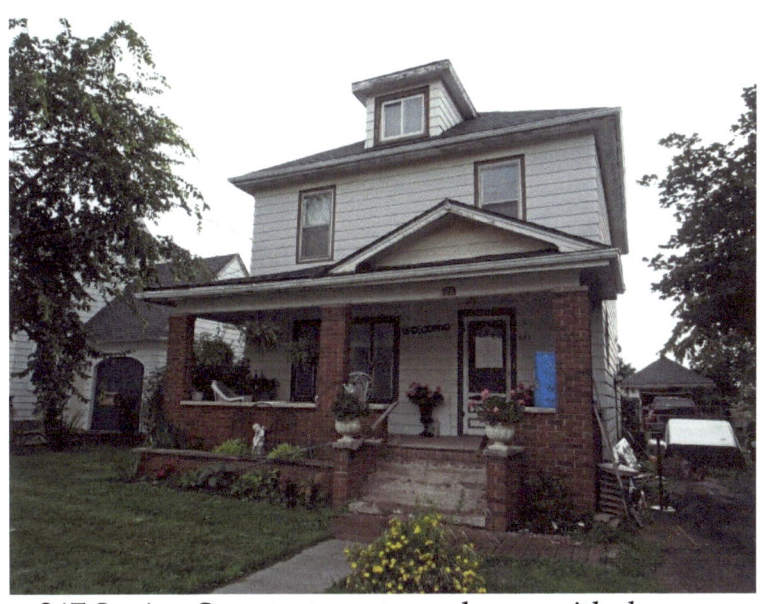

247 Station Street – two storey home with dormer, pediment

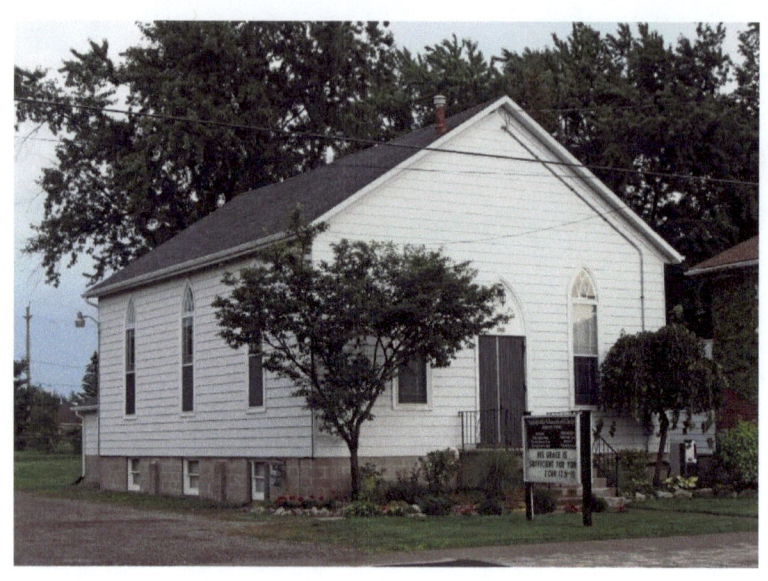

246 Station Street – Smithville Church of Christ – lancet windows

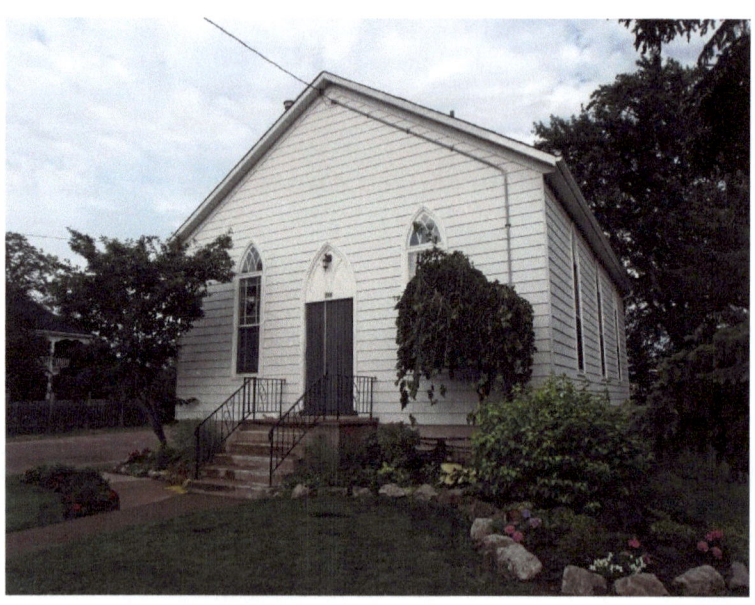

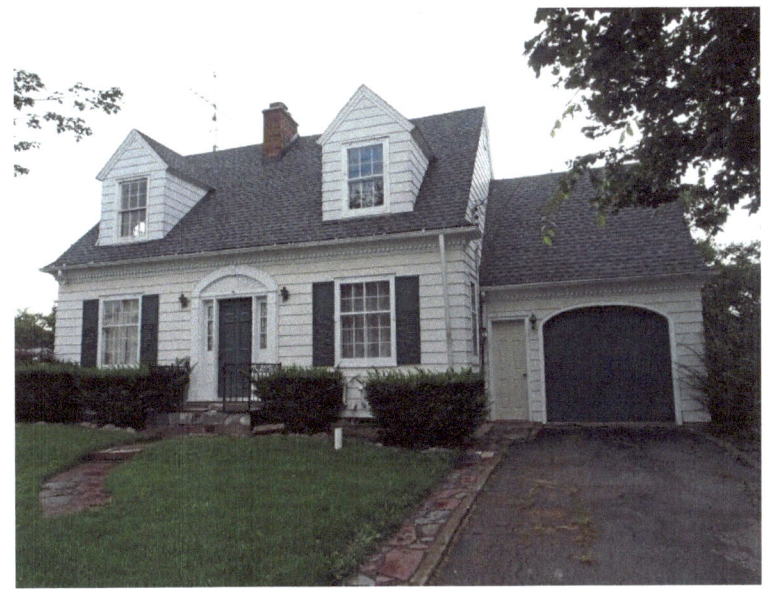

Station Street – dormers, sidelights with semi-circular pediment above door

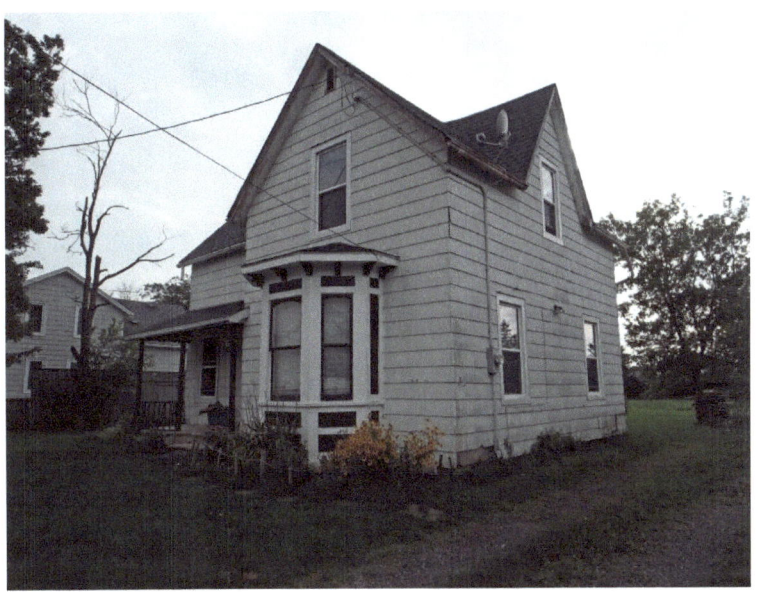

233 Station Street – Gothic – bay window

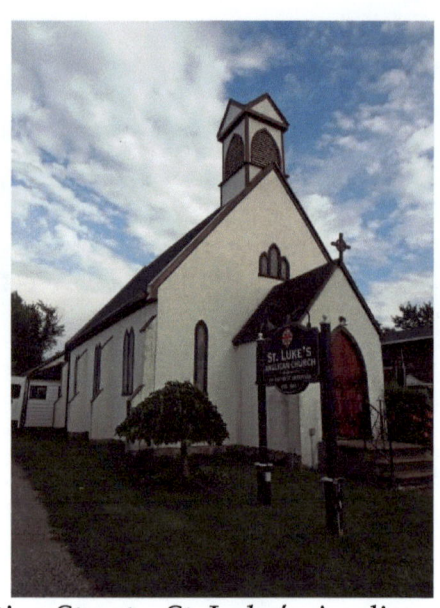

216 Station Street – St. Luke's Anglican Church

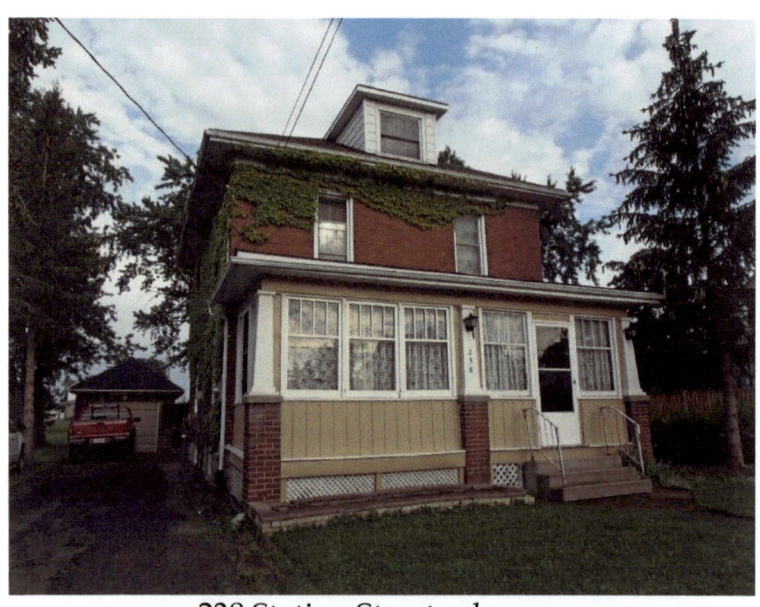

238 Station Street - dormer

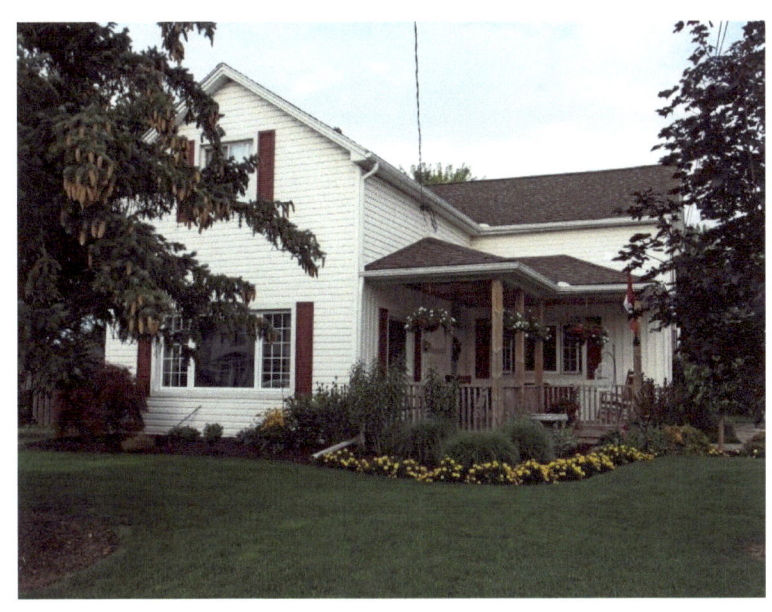

224 Station Street

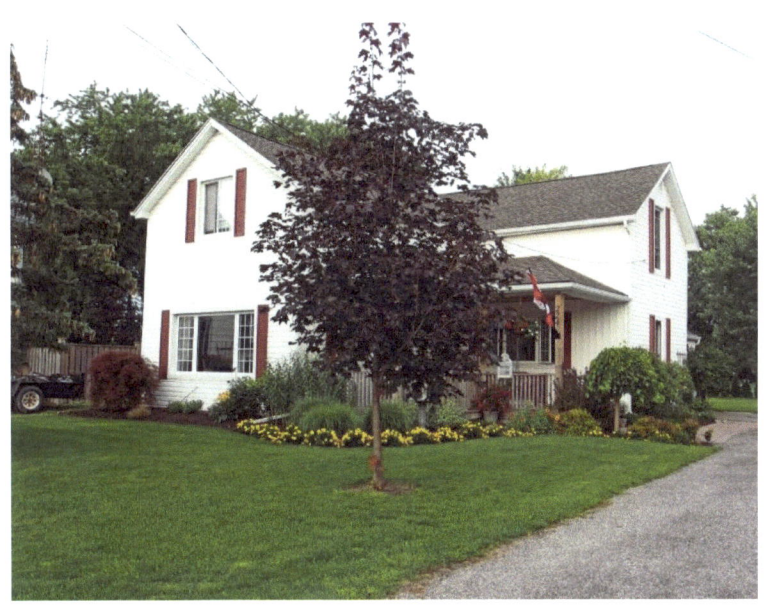

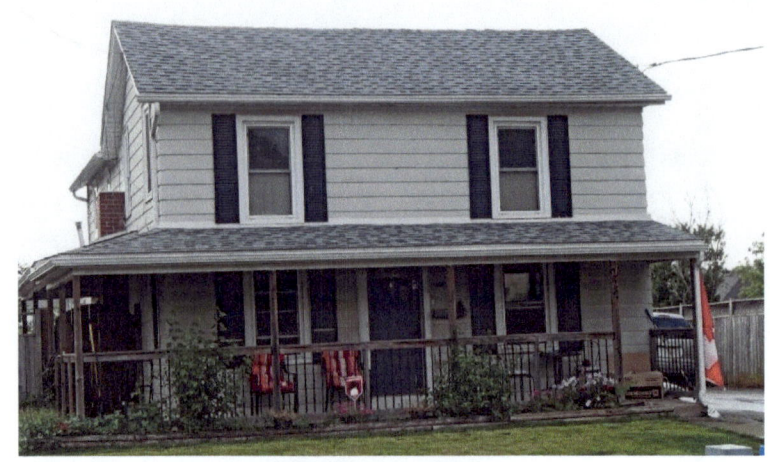

227 Station Street

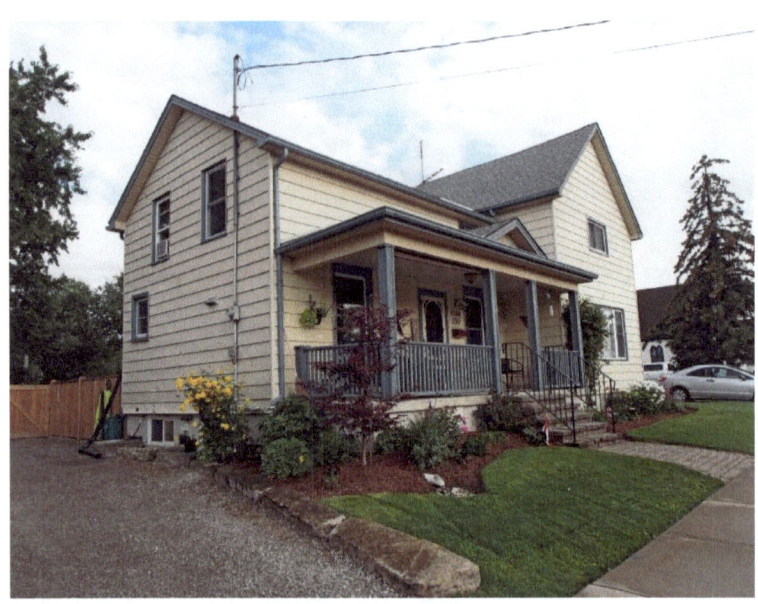

230 Station Street

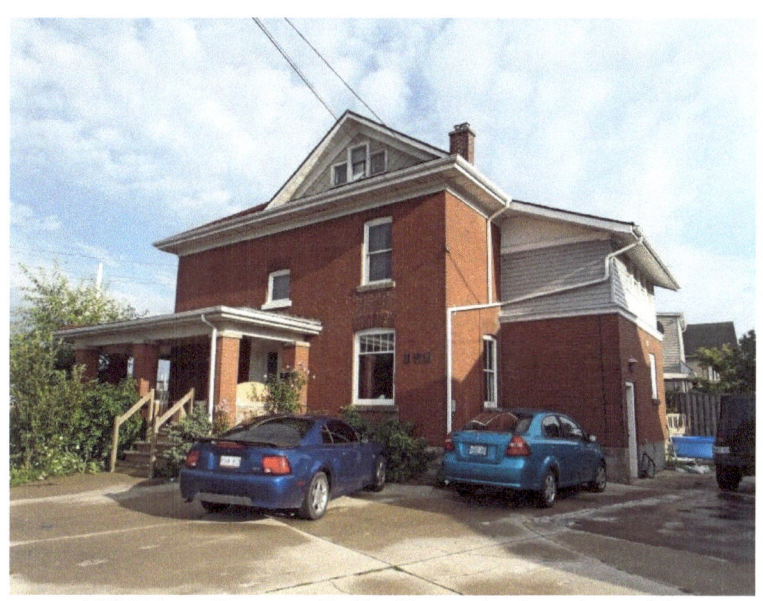

100 West Street – Palladian window in gable

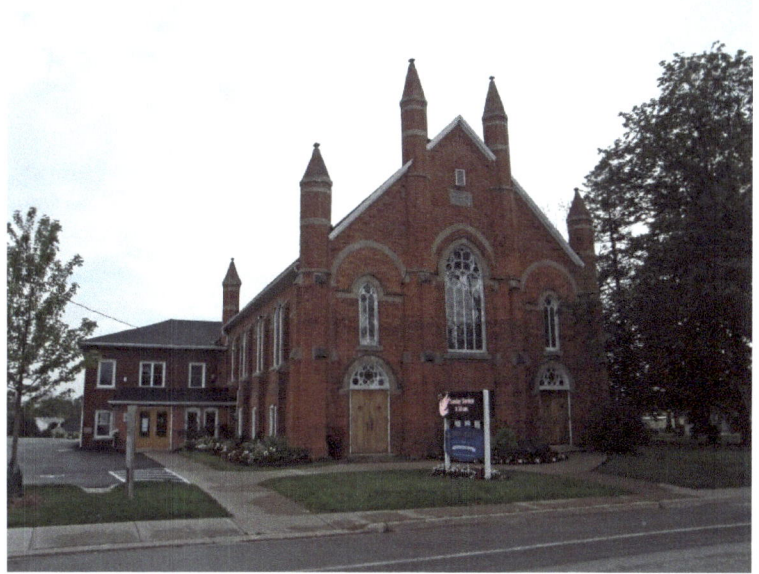

116 West Street – Smithville United Church – 1882 – Gothic Revival – buttresses with finials, dichromatic brickwork, muntins in the windows

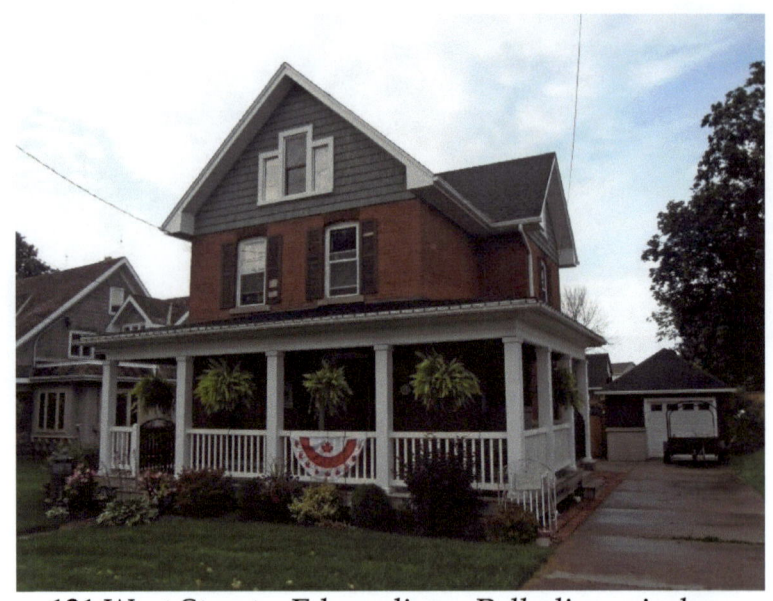

121 West Street – Edwardian – Palladian window

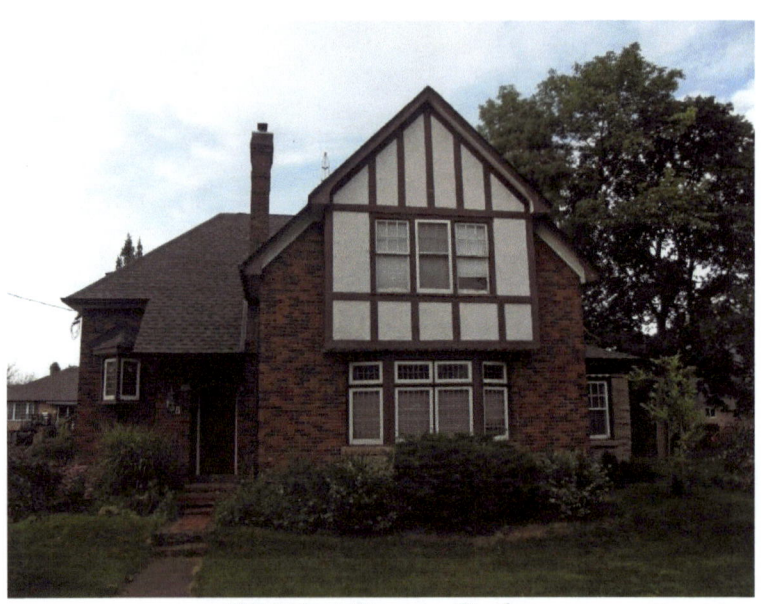

135 West Street - Tudor

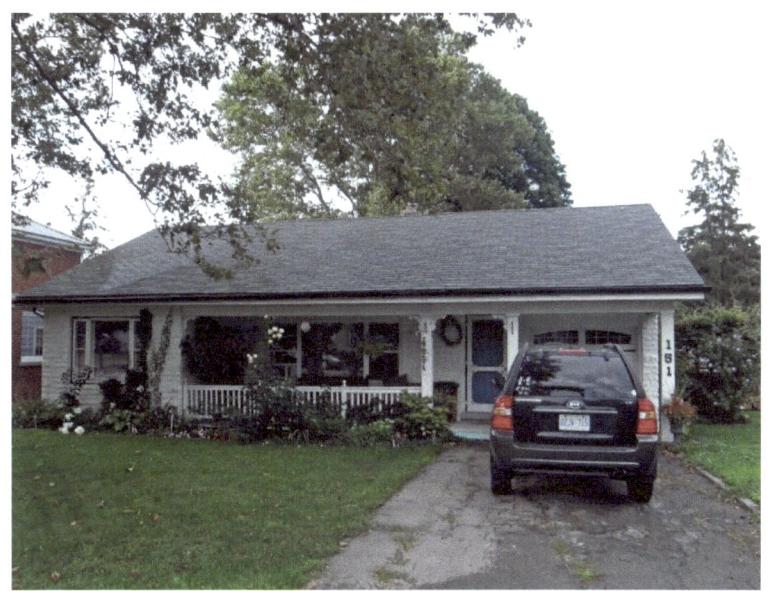

151 West Street – Regency Cottage

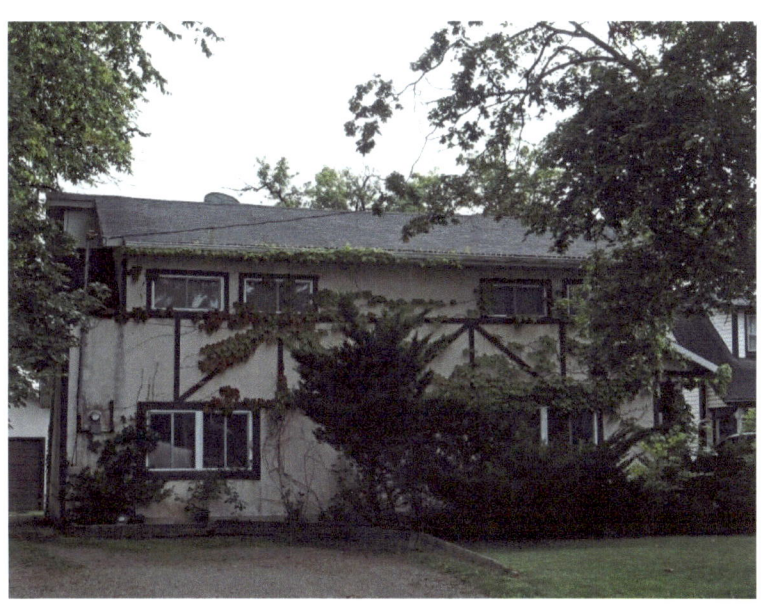

West Street

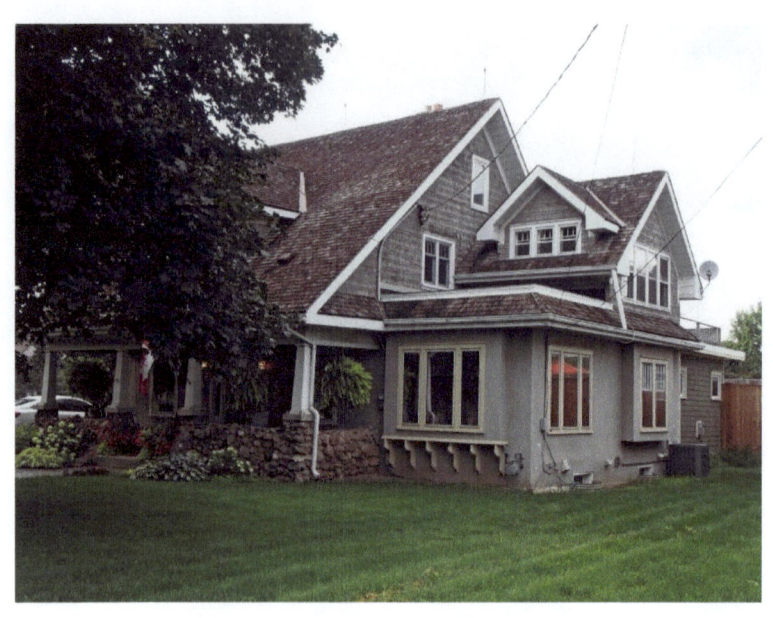

125 West Street - dormers

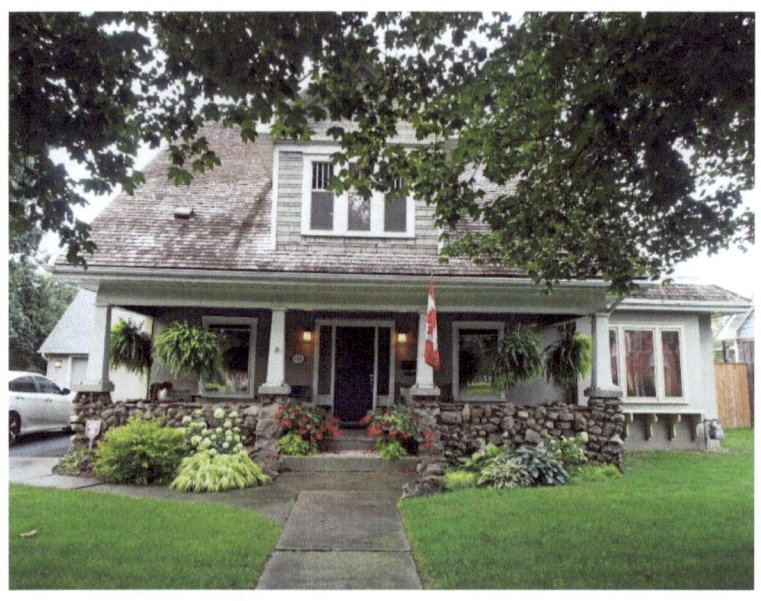

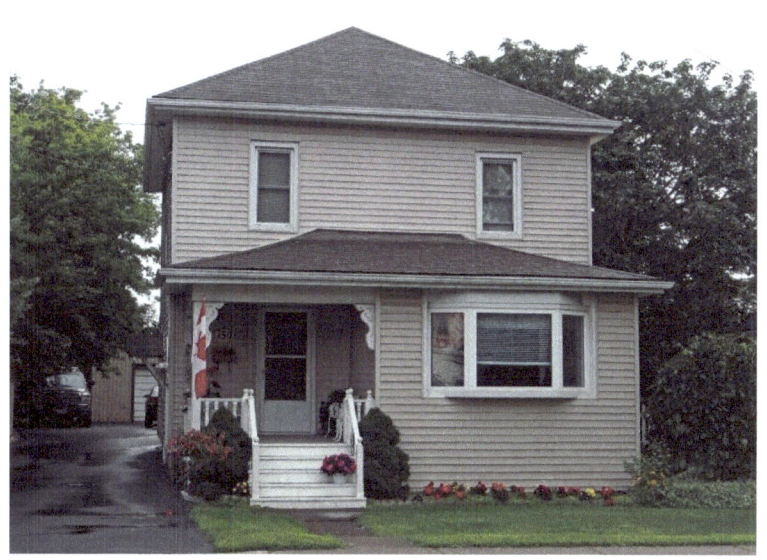

150 West Street – hipped roof

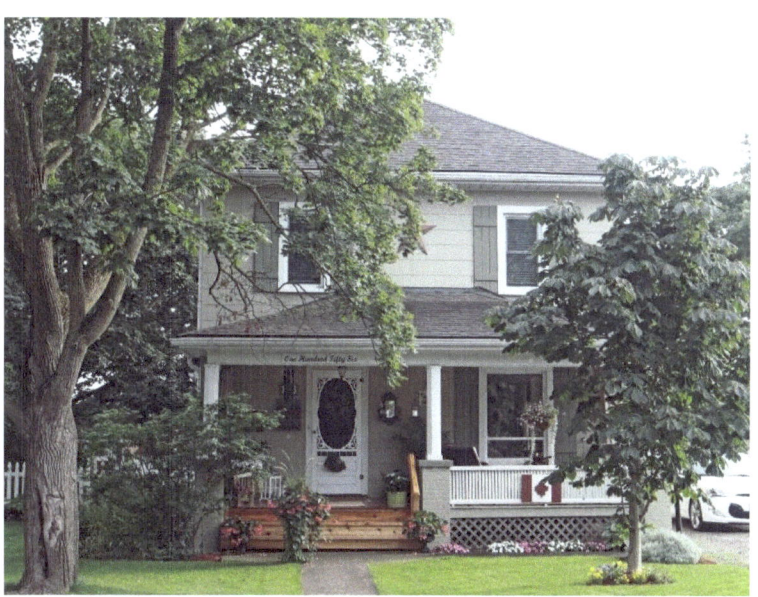

156 West Street

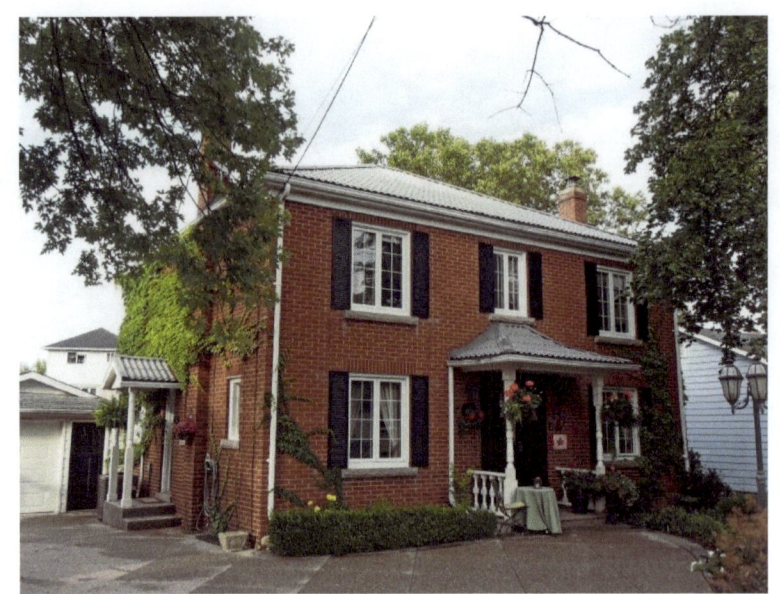

157 West Street – balanced façade

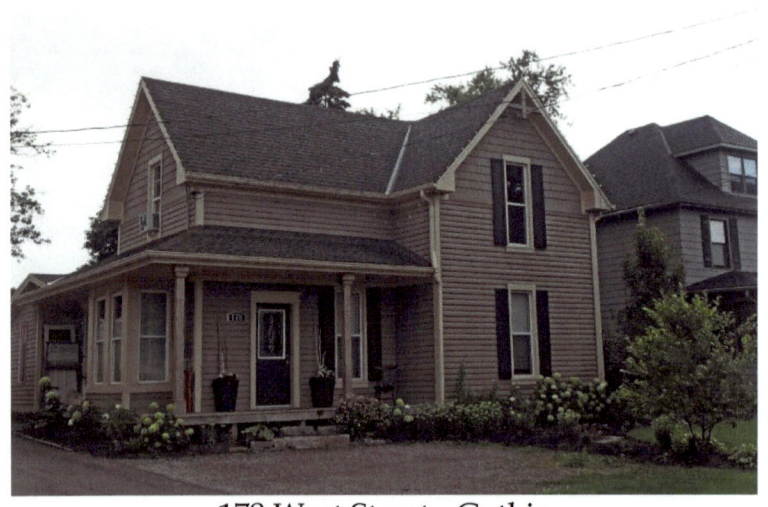

178 West Street - Gothic

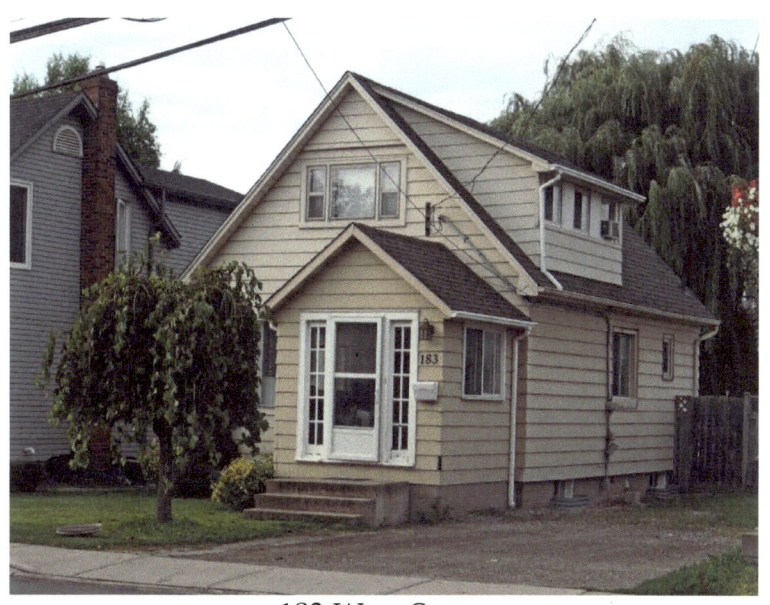

183 West Street

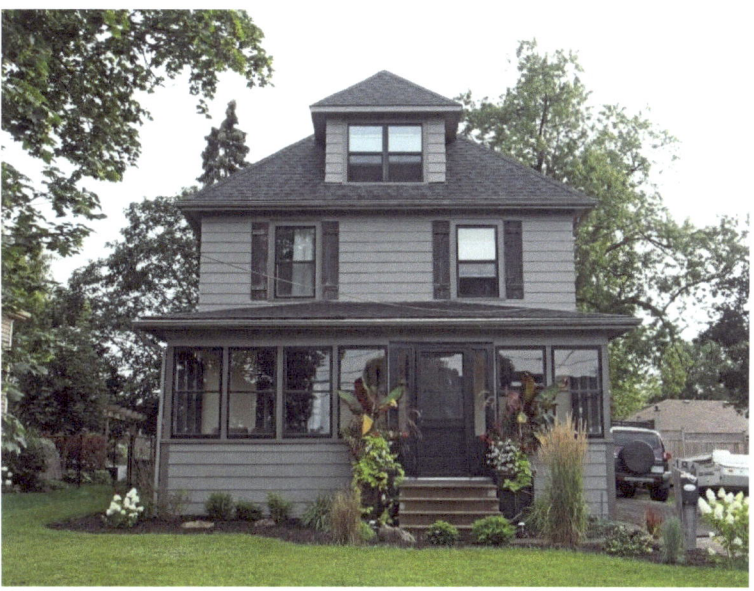

184 West Street – two-storey house with dormer in attic

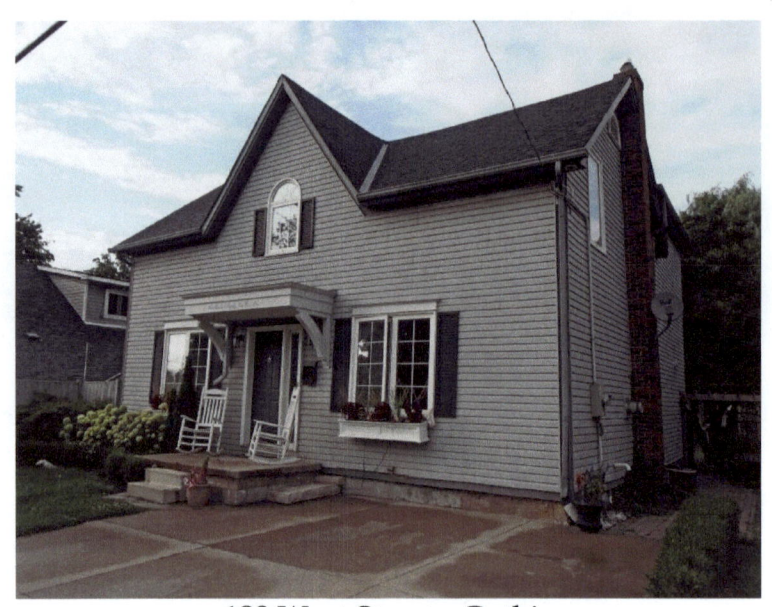

189 West Street - Gothic

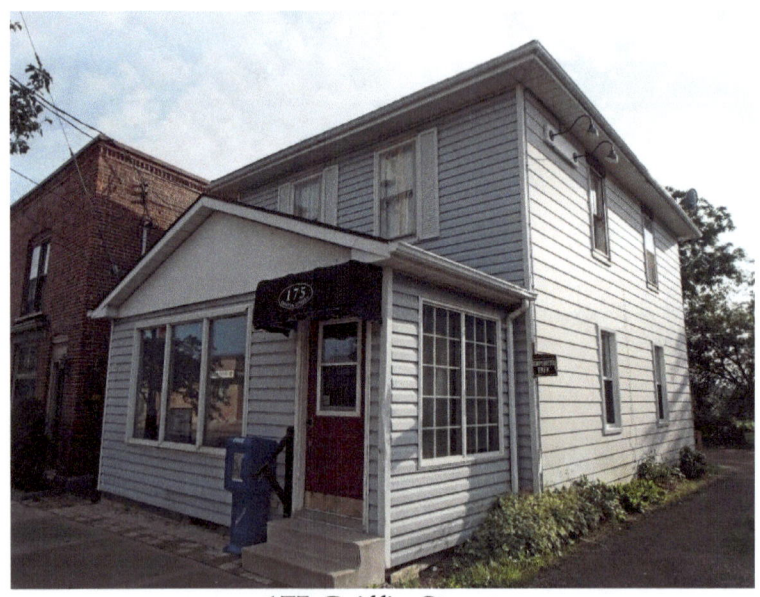

175 Griffin Street

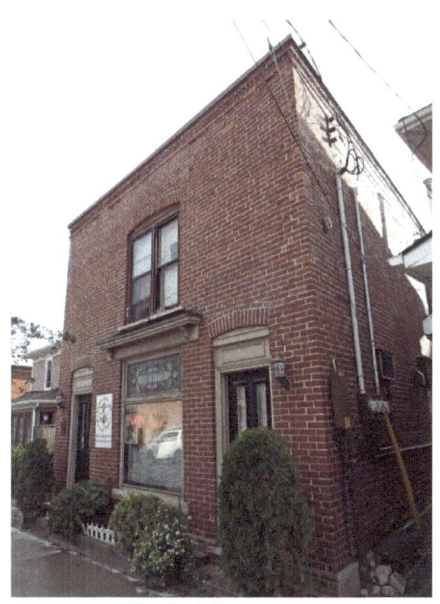

171 Griffin Street

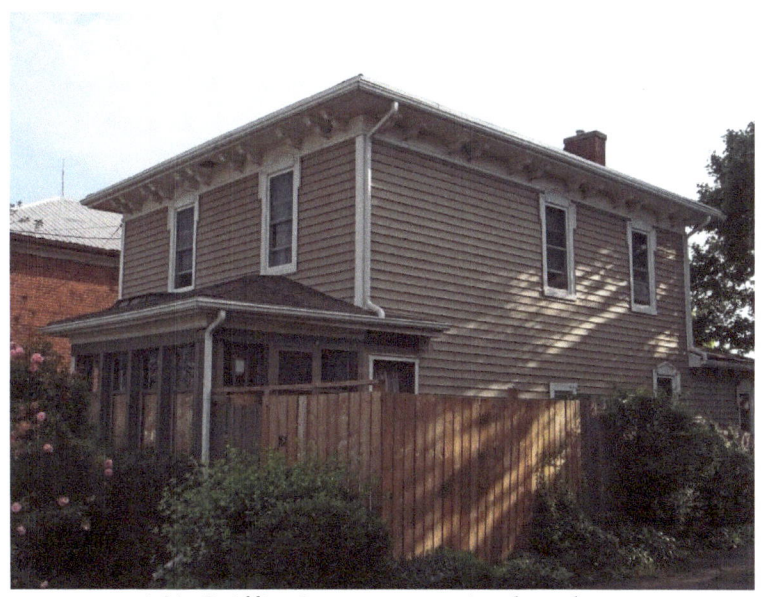

161 Griffin Street – cornice brackets

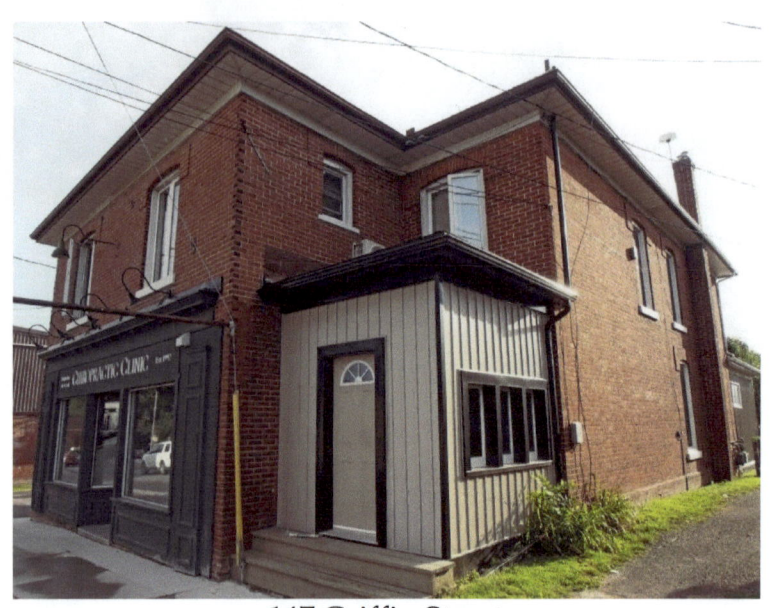

147 Griffin Street

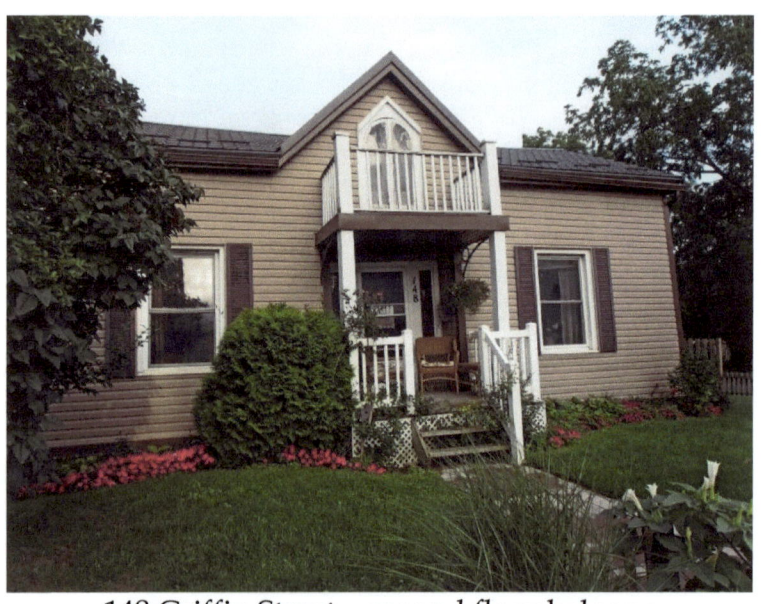

148 Griffin Street – second floor balcony

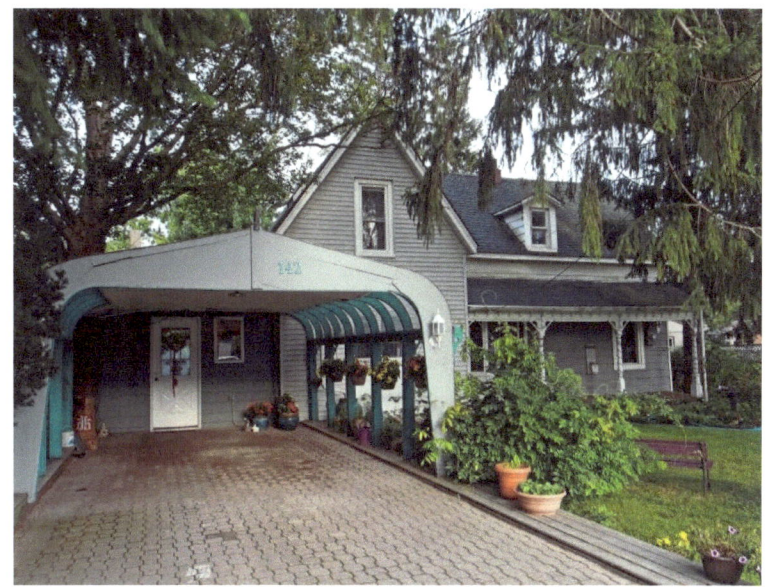

142 Griffin Street

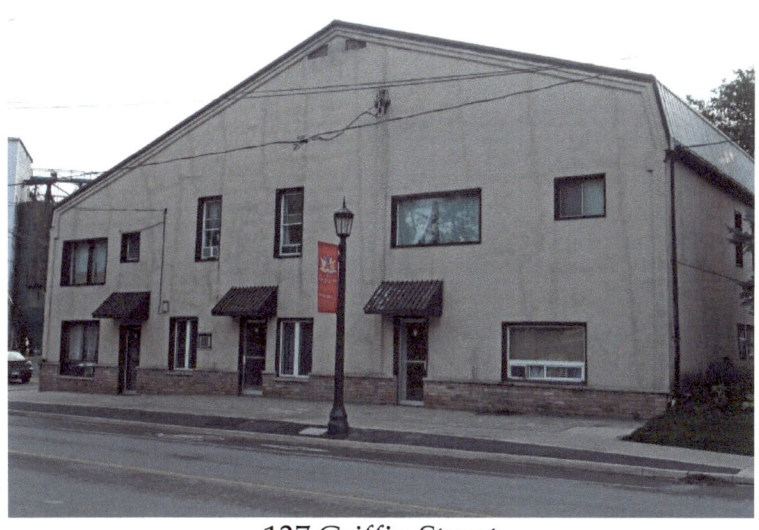

137 Griffin Street

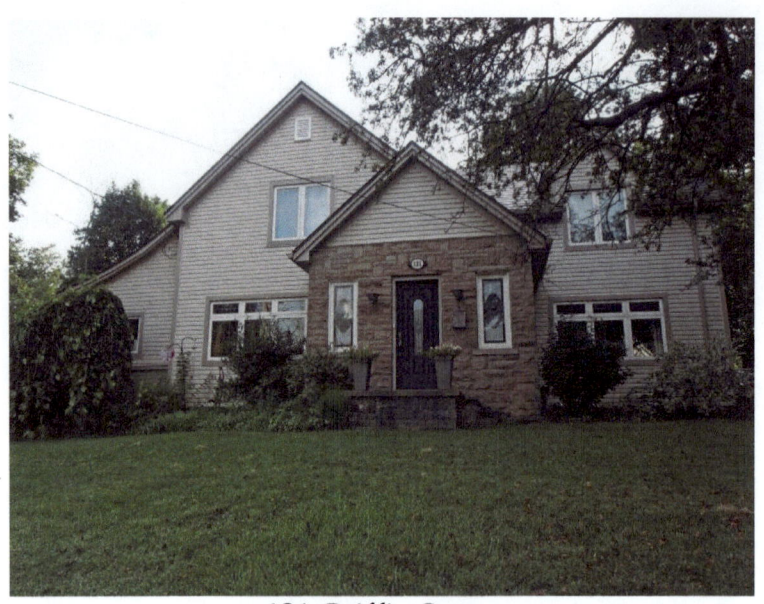

121 Griffin Street

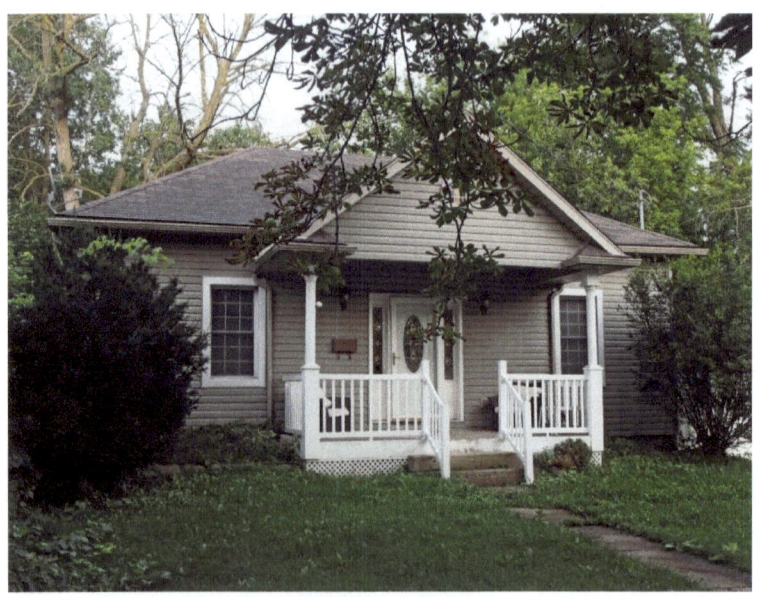

Griffin Street

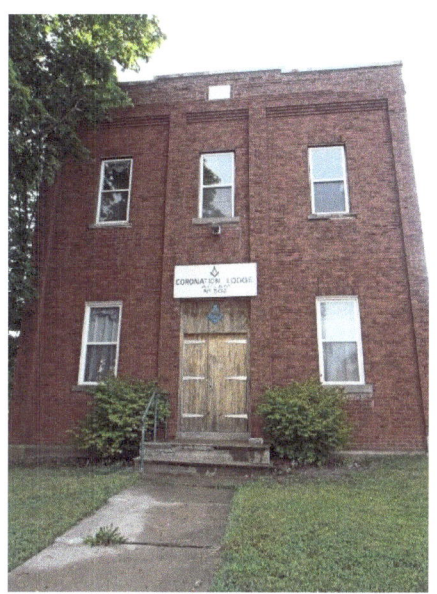

113 Griffin Street – Coronation Lodge

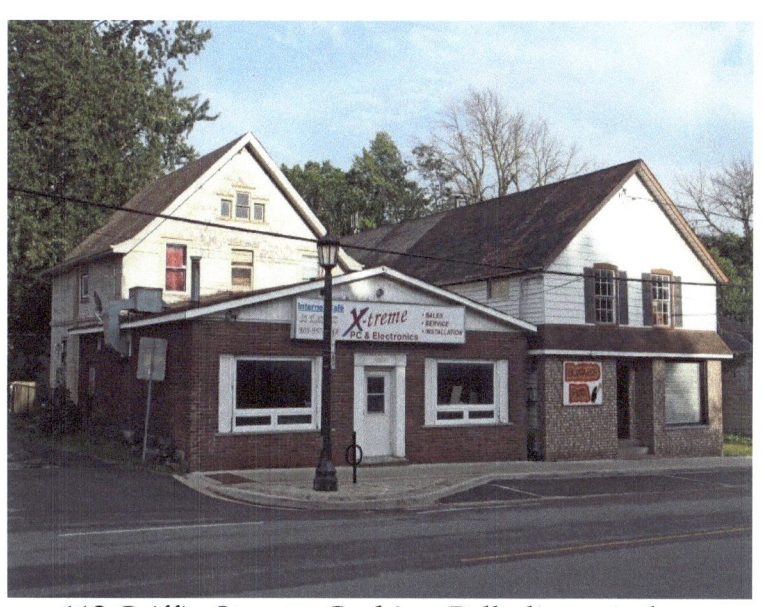

112 Griffin Street – Gothic – Palladian window

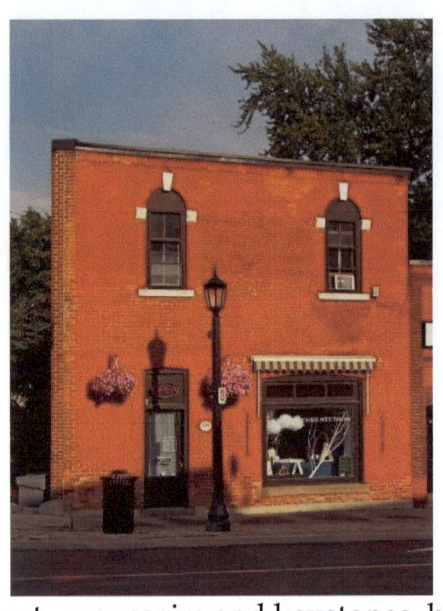

104 Griffin Street – voussoirs and keystones, blind transoms

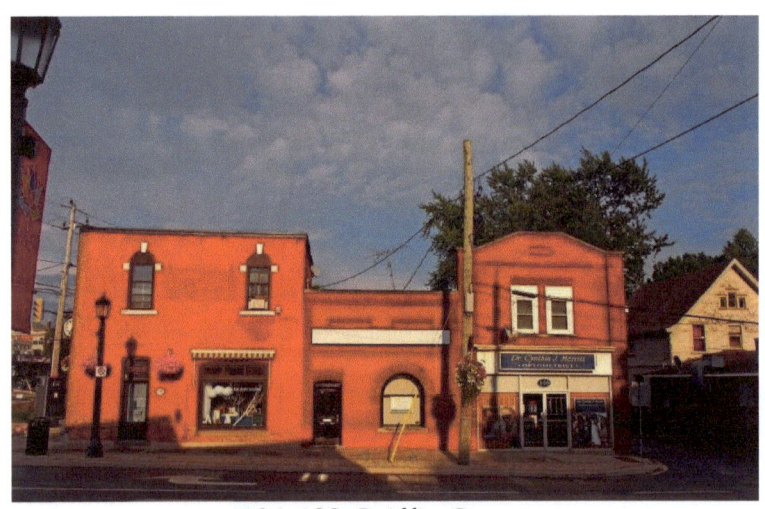

104-108 Griffin Street

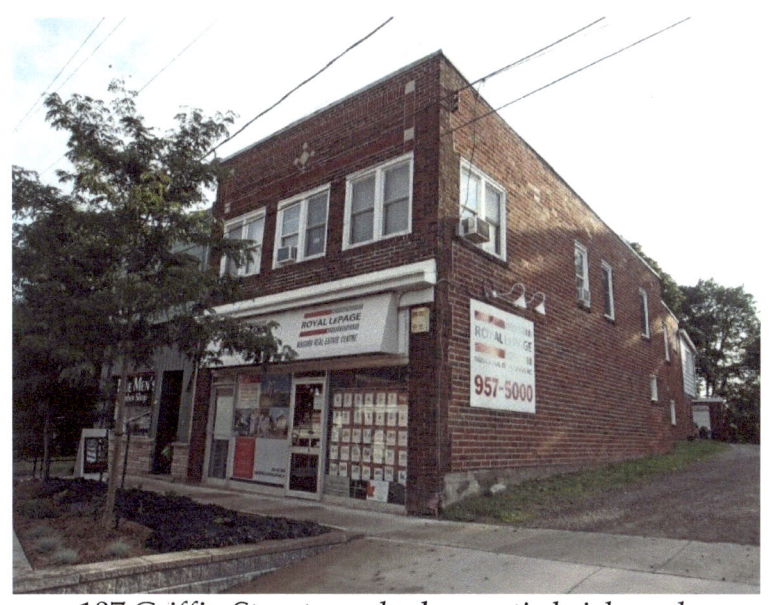

107 Griffin Street – polychromatic brickwork

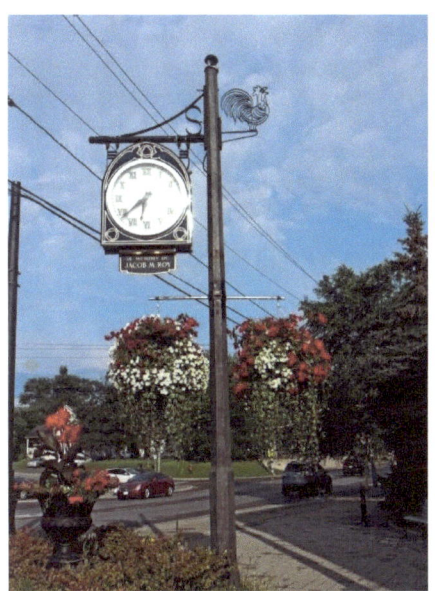
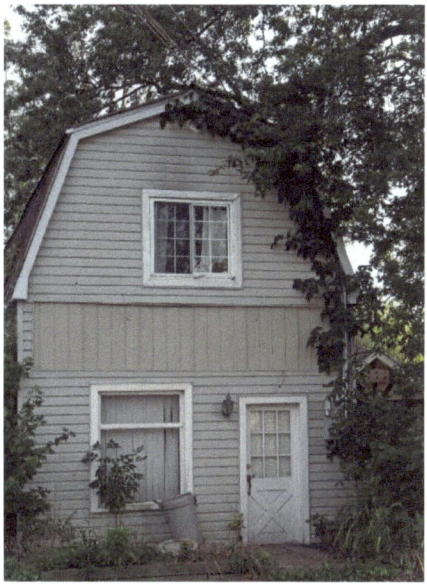

Town clock

St. Catharine Street
Neo-Colonial – gambrel roof

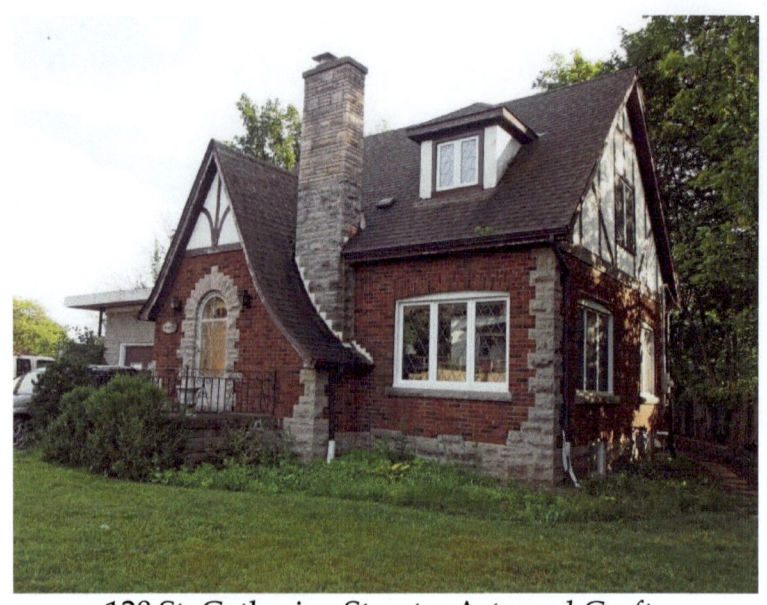

120 St. Catharine Street – Arts and Crafts

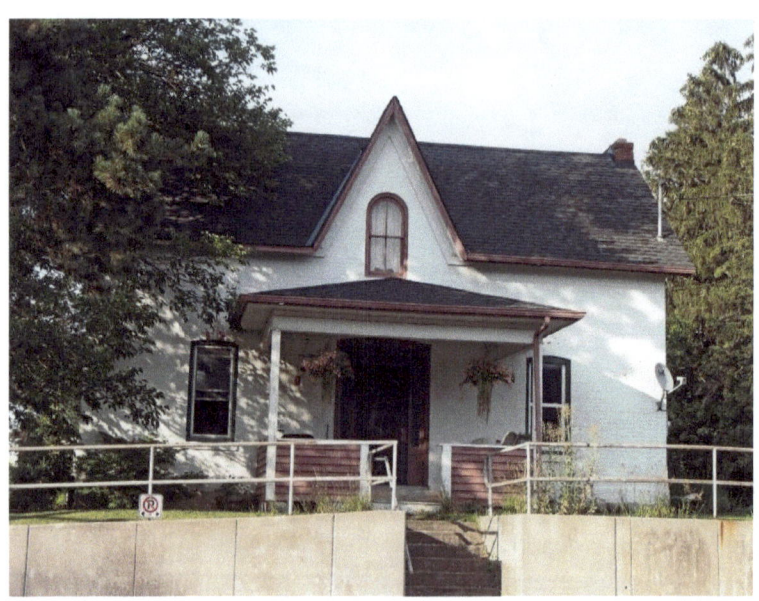

St. Catharine Street - Gothic

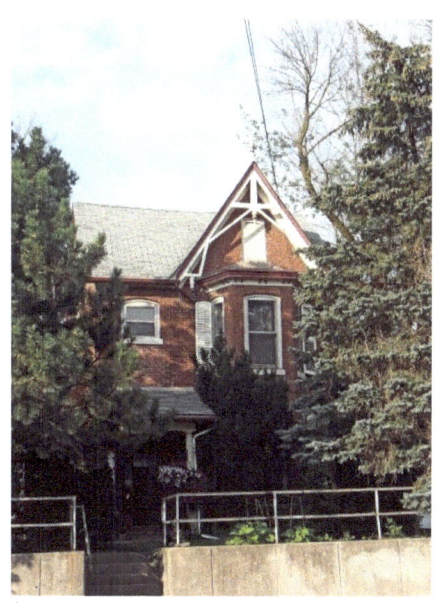

131 St. Catharine Street – verge board trim on gable

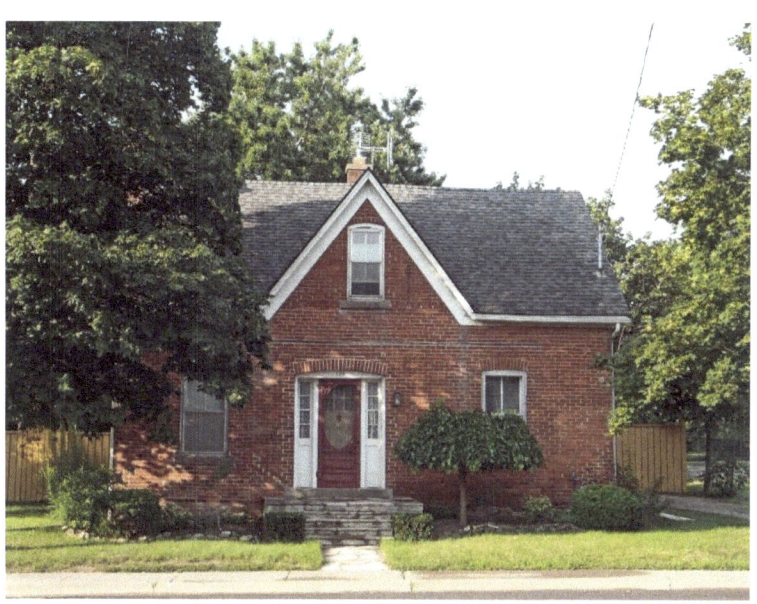

139 St. Catharine Street - Gothic

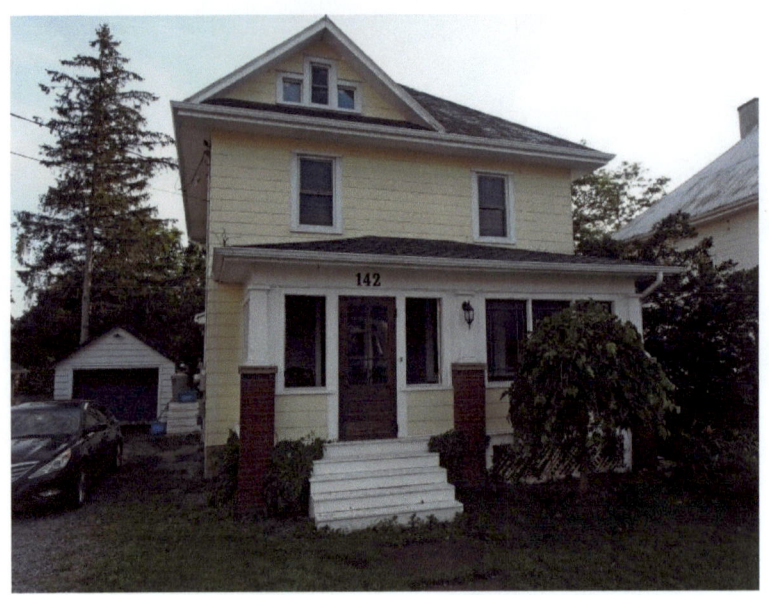
142 St. Catharine Street – Palladian window

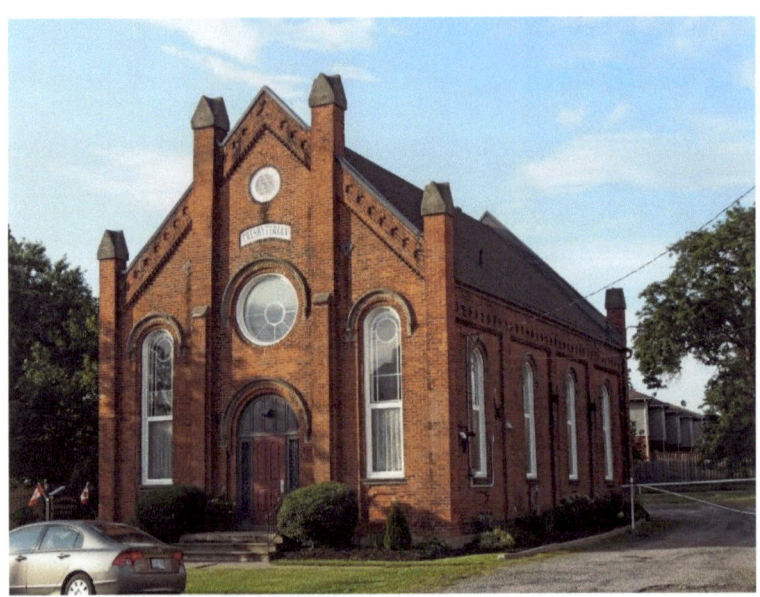
143 St. Catharine Street – Smithville Presbyterian Church – Romanesque style, buttresses, decorative brickwork, rose window, sidelights and blind transom

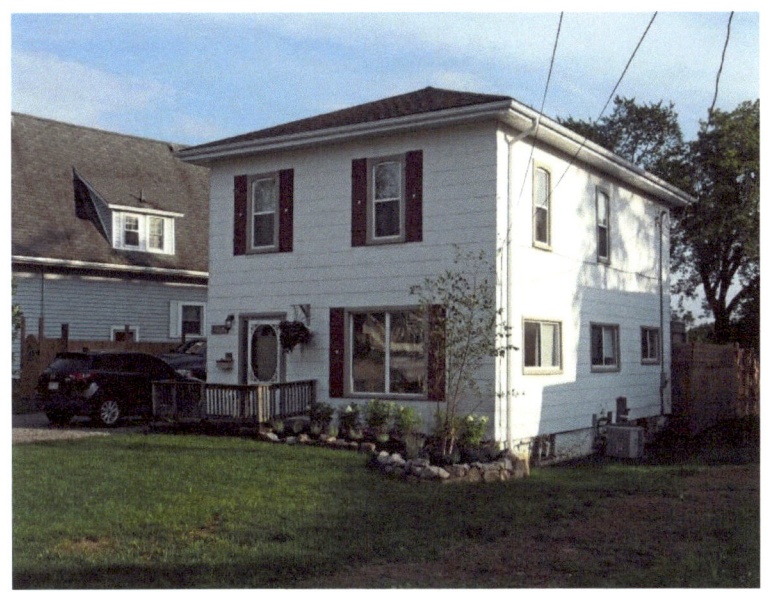

150 St. Catharine Street – hipped roof

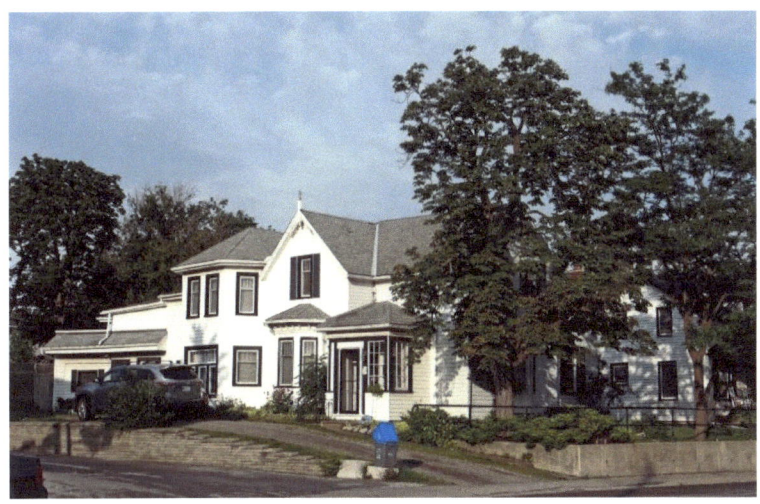

153 St. Catharine Street – verge board and finial on gable, bay window

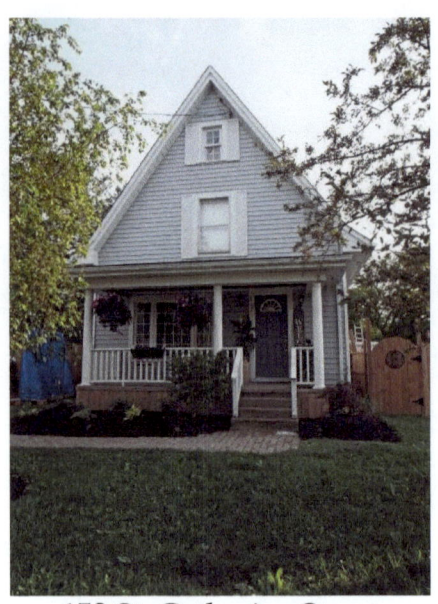

152 St. Catharine Street

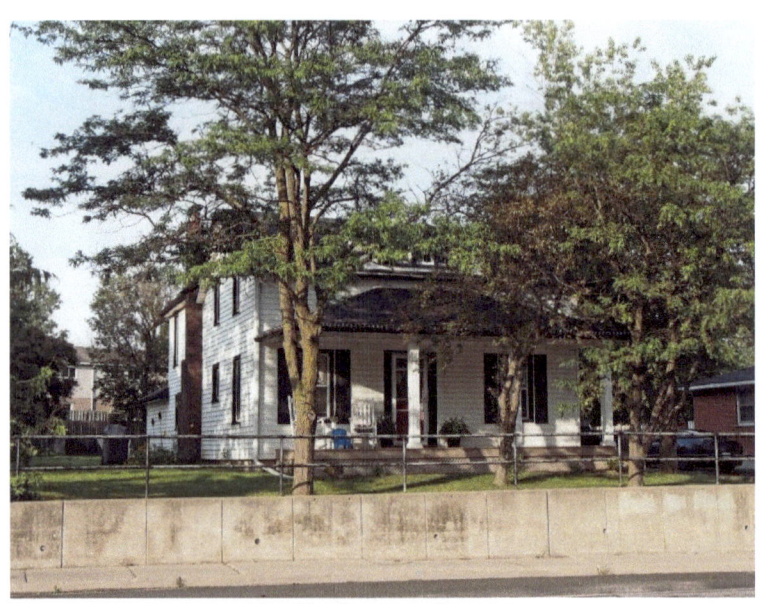

St. Catharine Street

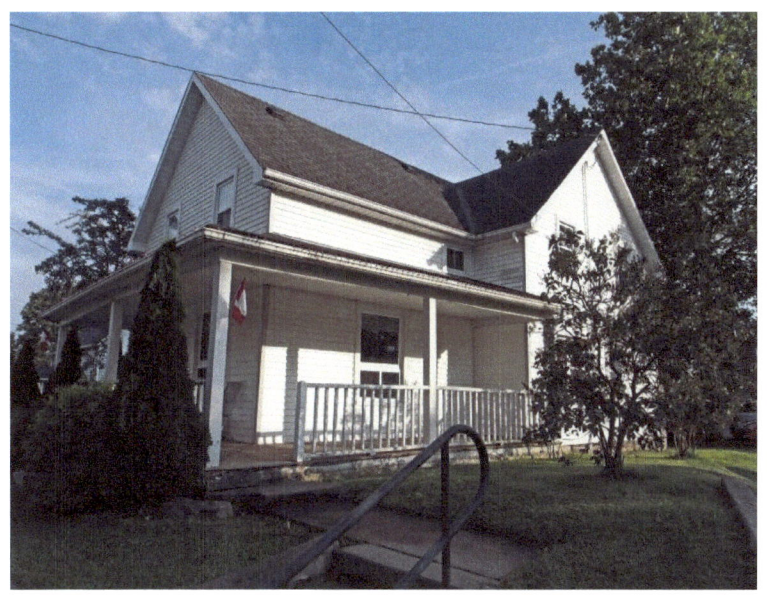
160 St. Catharine Street

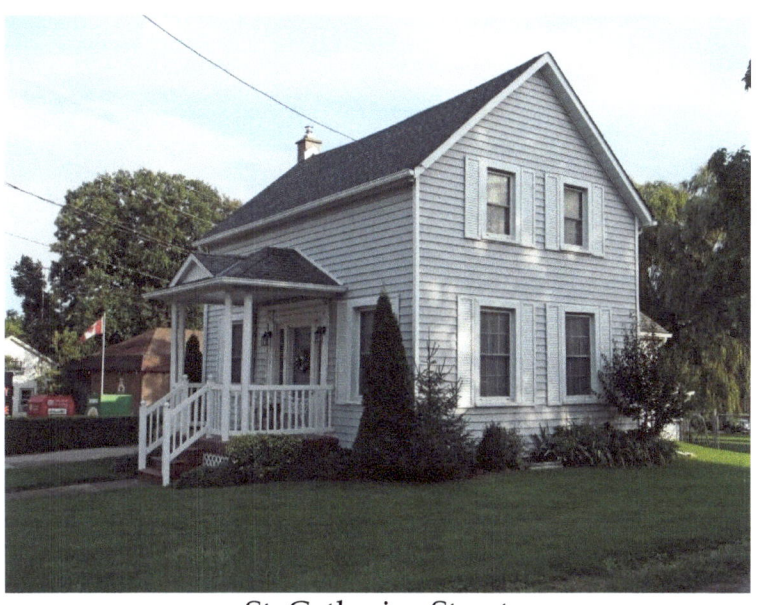
St. Catharine Street

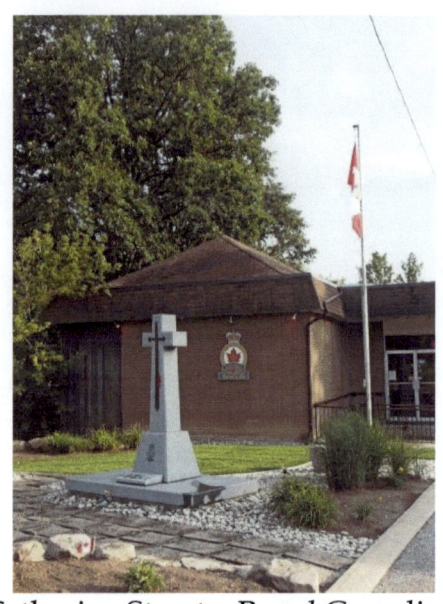

172 St. Catharine Street – Royal Canadian Legion

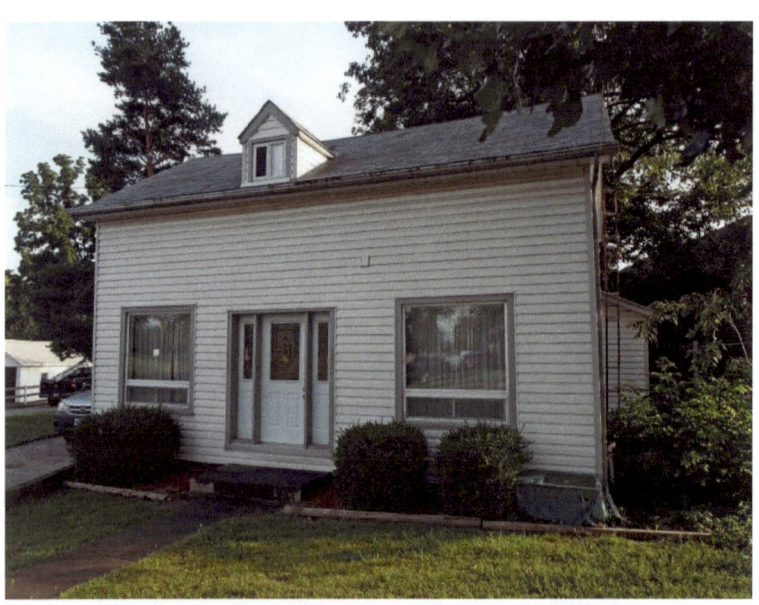

St. Catharine Street – dormer, sidelights

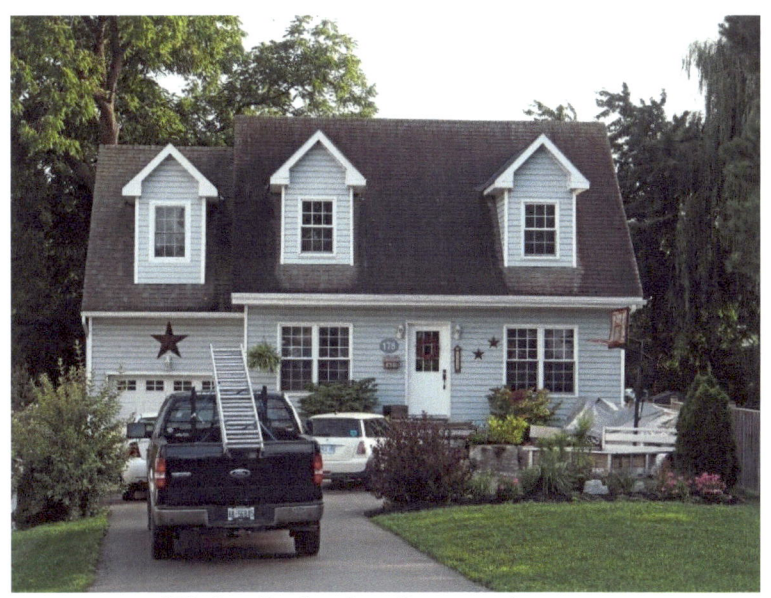
178 St. Catharine Street - dormers

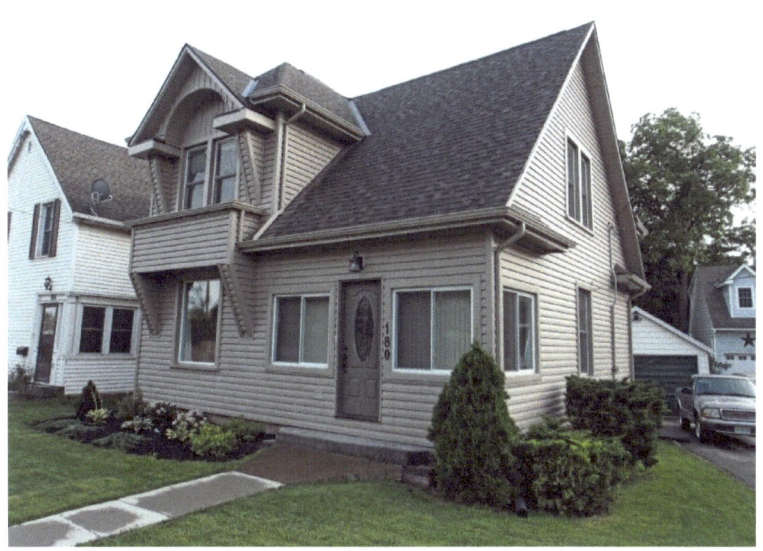
180 St. Catharine Street

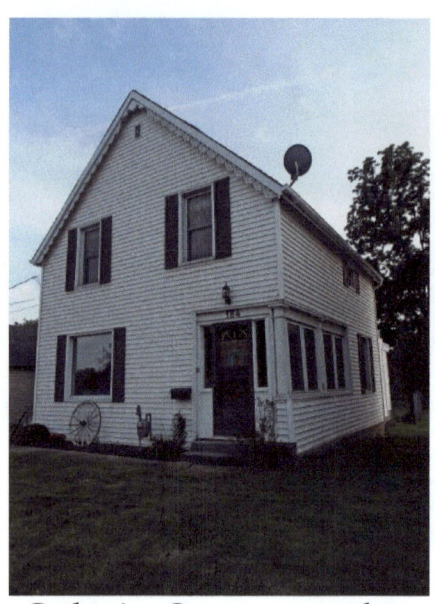

184 St. Catharine Street – verge board trim

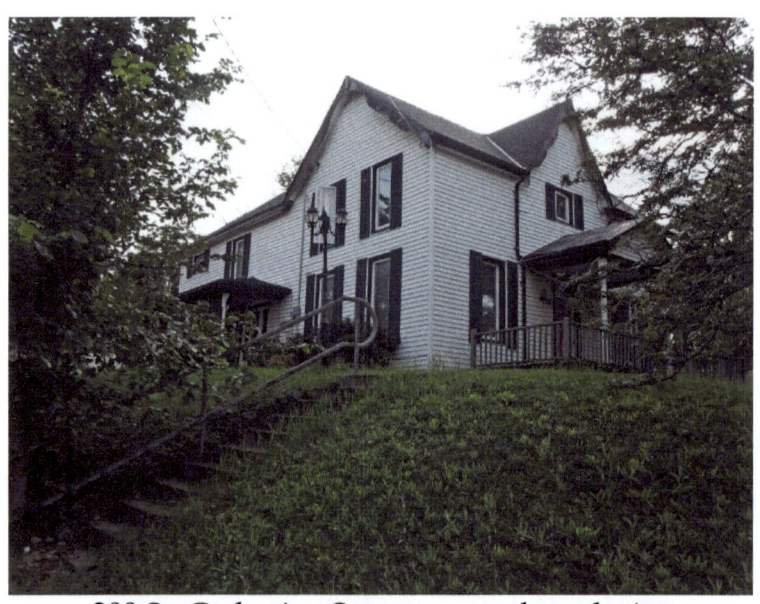

200 St. Catharine Street - verge board trim

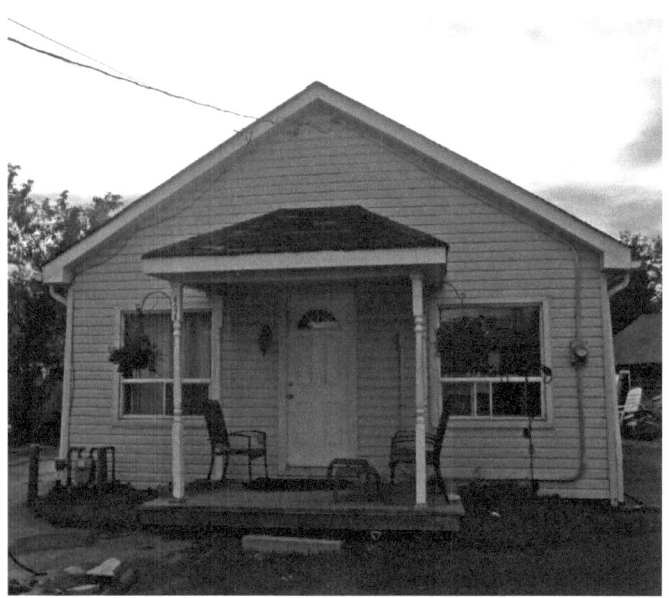

Canborough Street

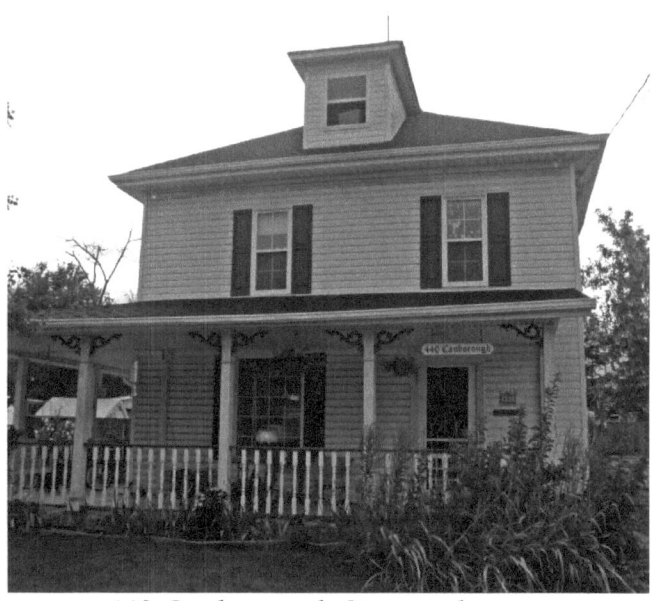

440 Canborough Street - dormer

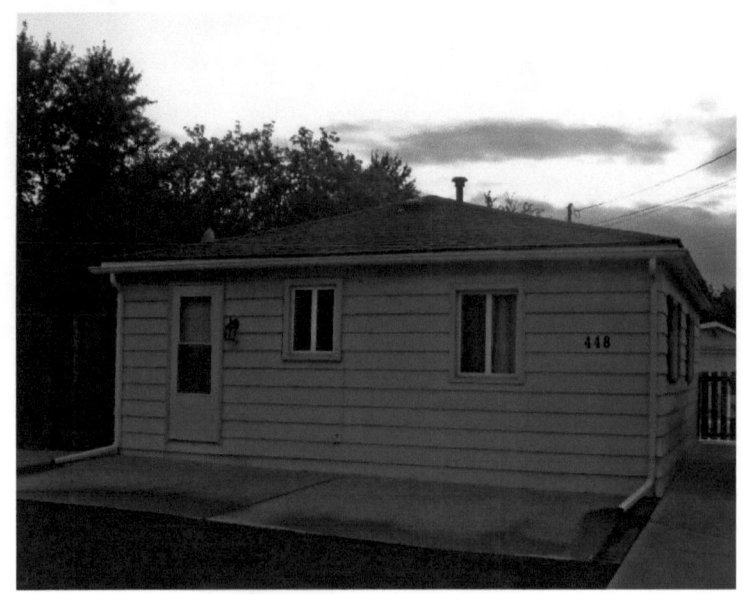

448 Canborough Street

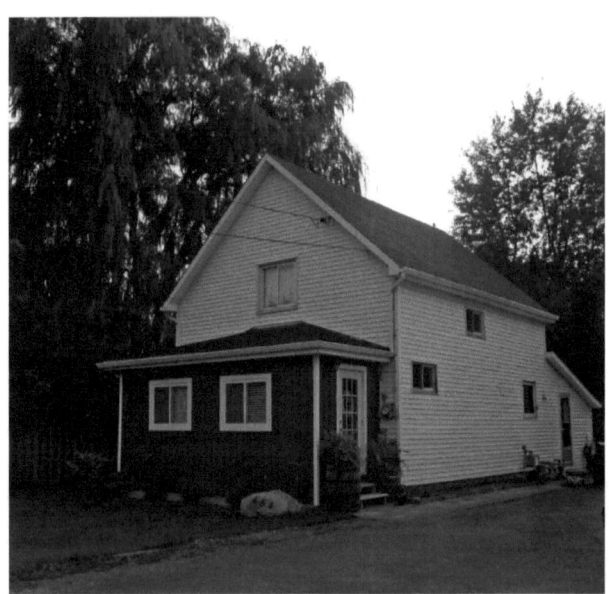

Canborough Street

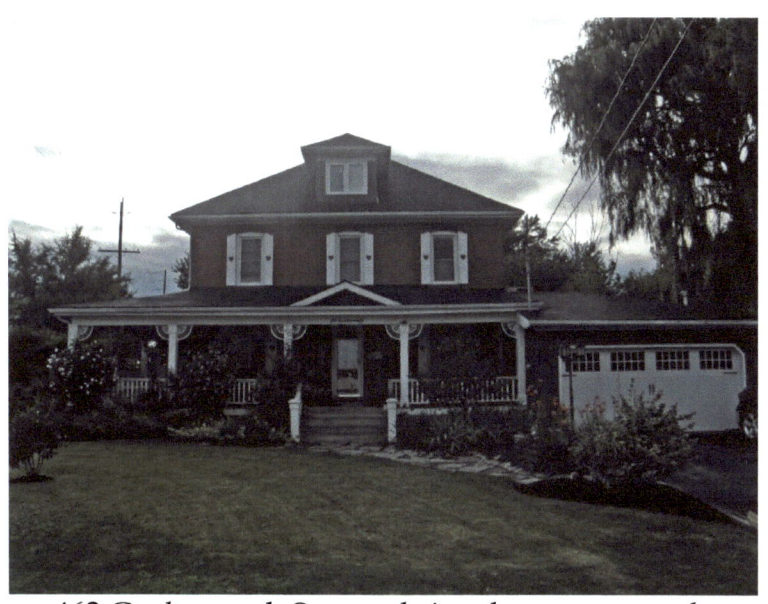

462 Canborough Street – bric-a-brac on veranda

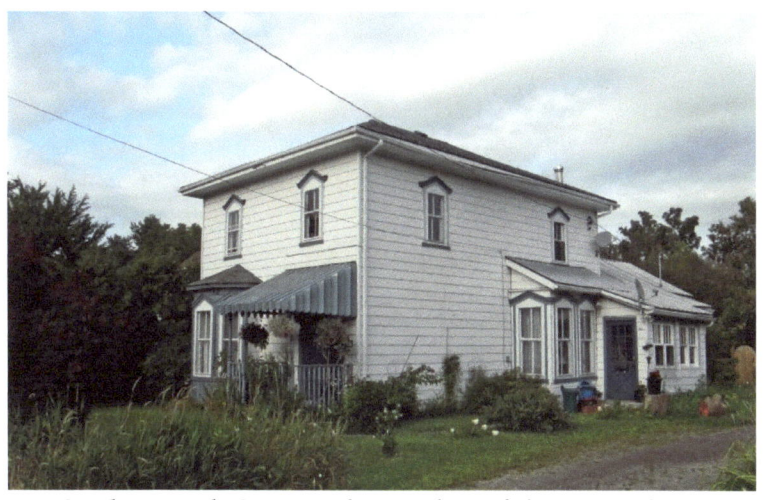

Canborough Street – hipped roof, bay windows

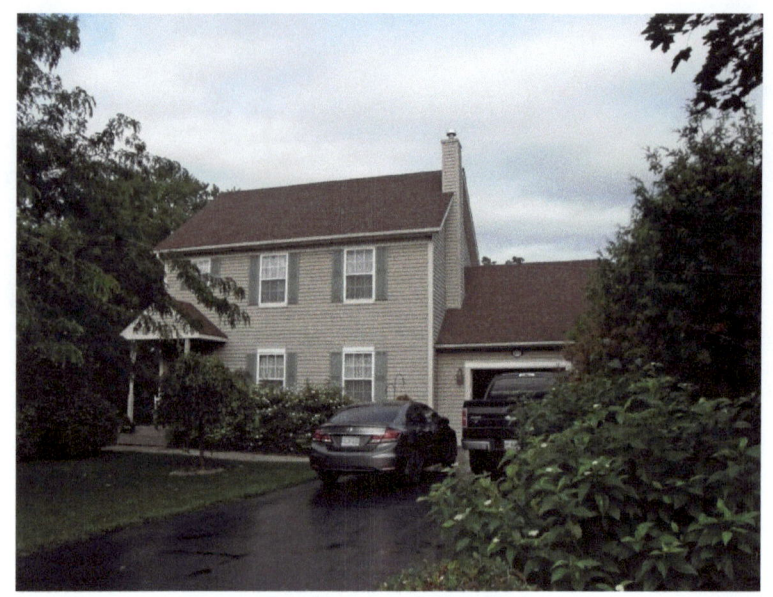

Canborough Street

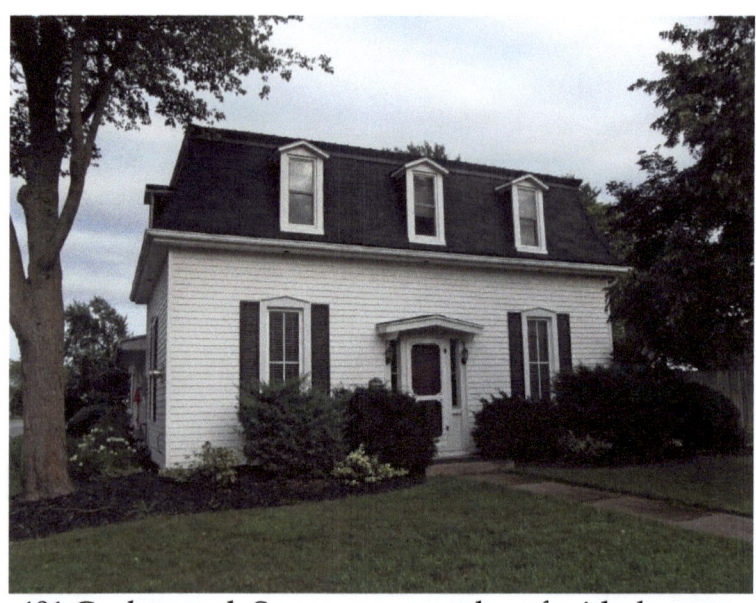

401 Canborough Street – mansard roof with dormers

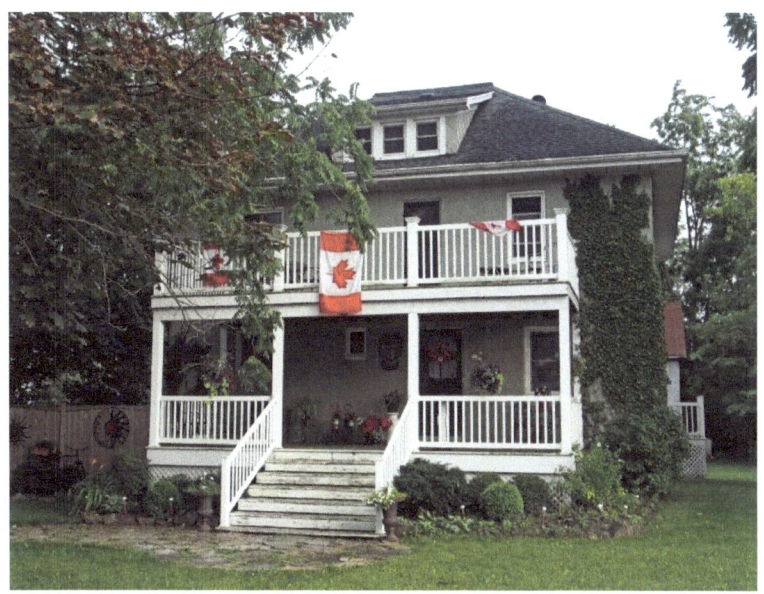

Canborough Street – second floor full width balcony, dormer

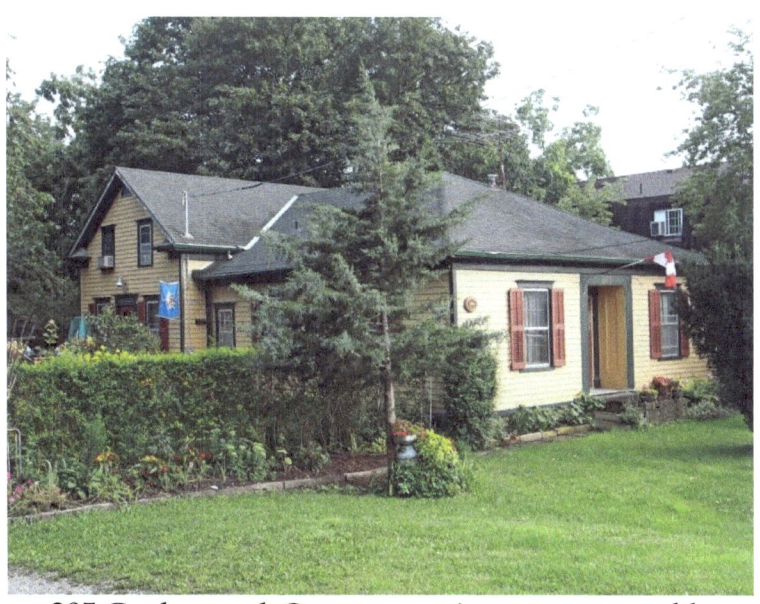

205 Canborough Street – cornice return on gable

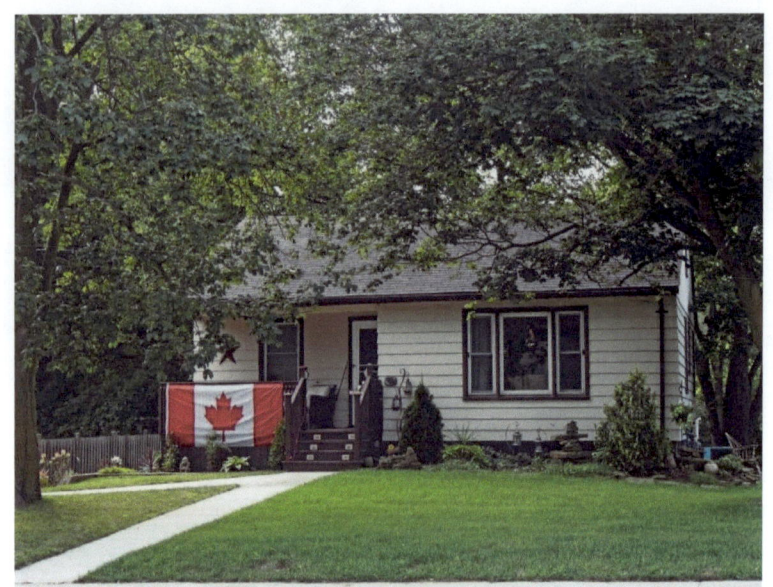

Canborough Street

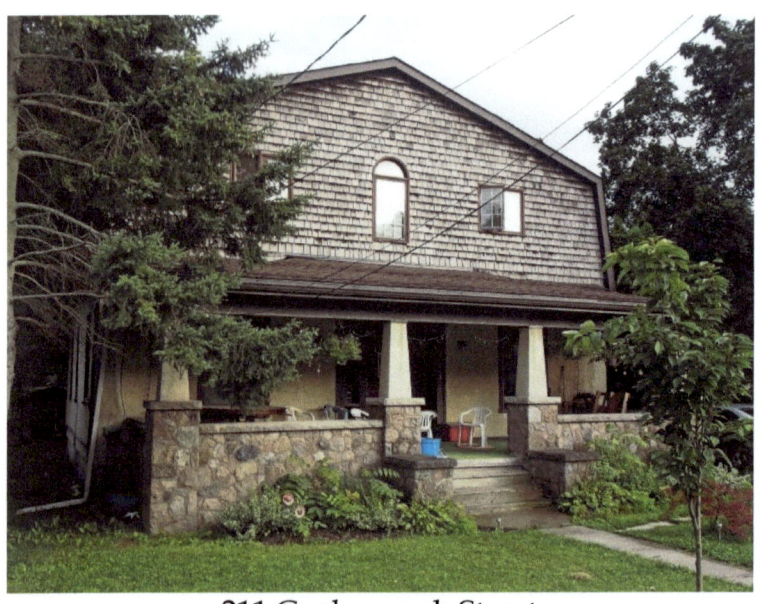

211 Canborough Street

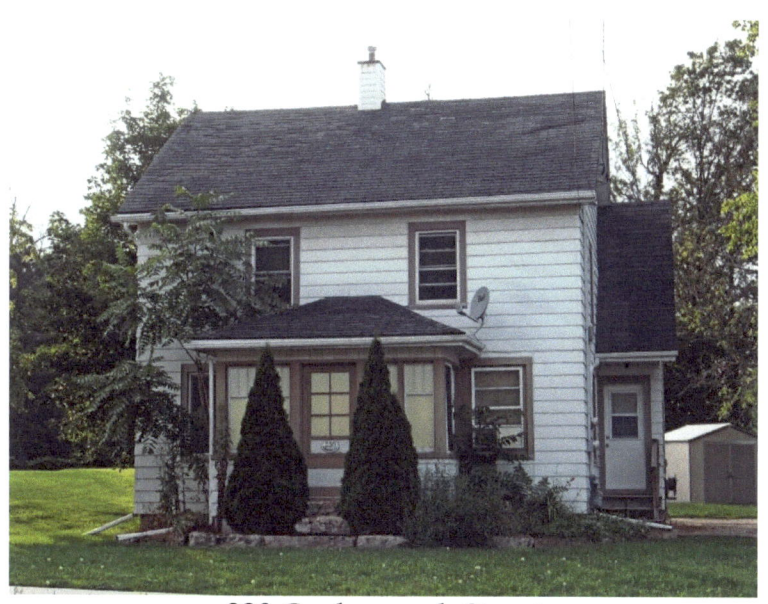

220 Canborough Street

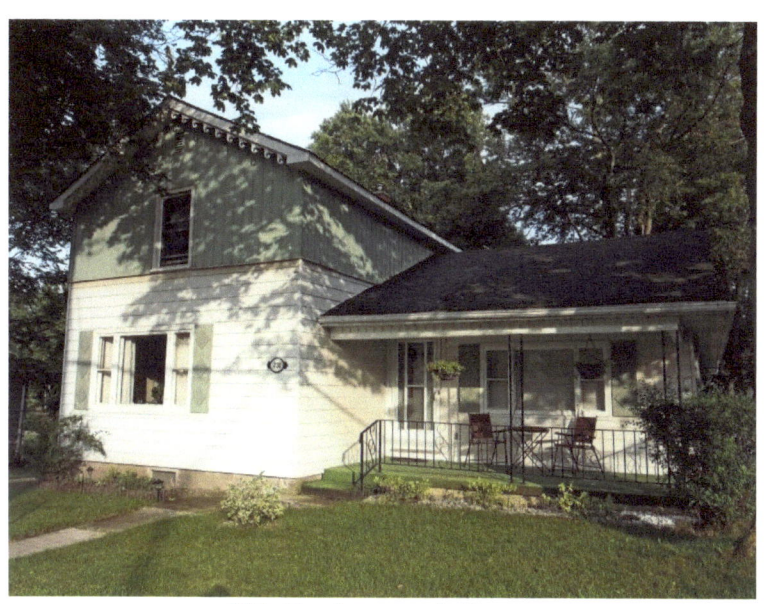

231 Canborough Street

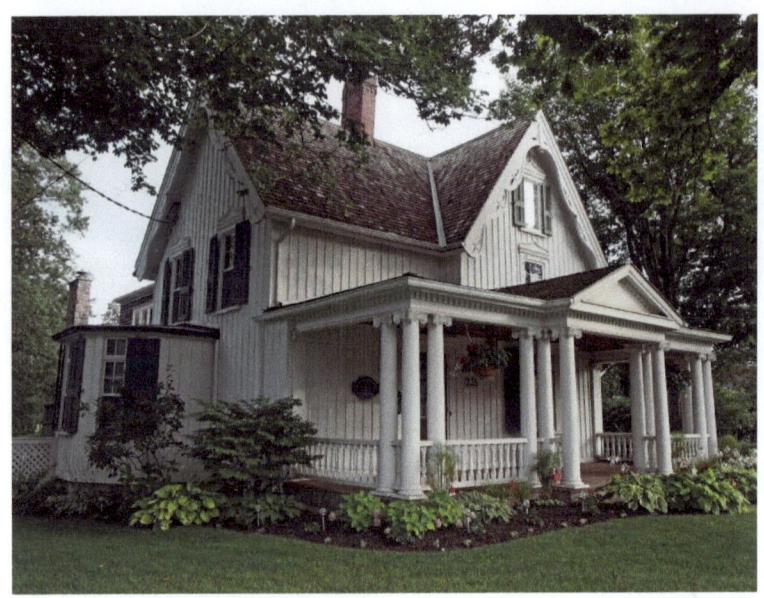

235 Canborough Street – Ionic capitals on the veranda pillars, pediment, verge board trim on gables, bay window

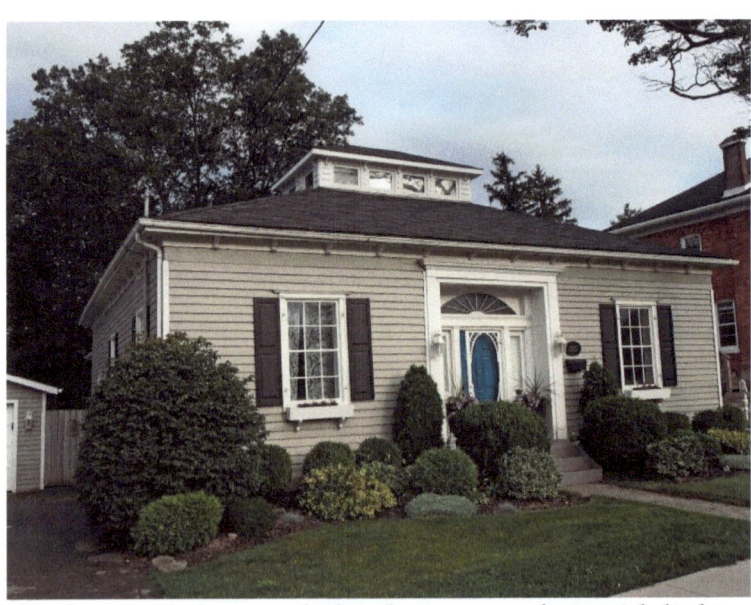

255 Canborough Street – belvedere on rooftop, sidelights and transom

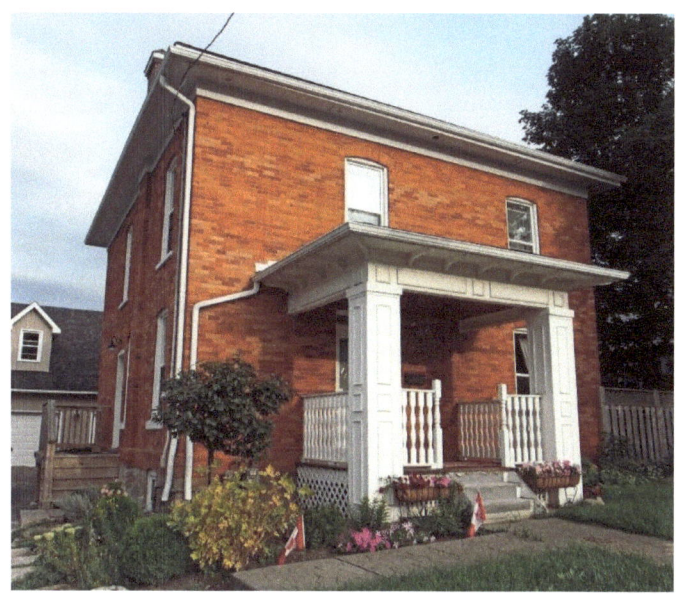

Canborough Street

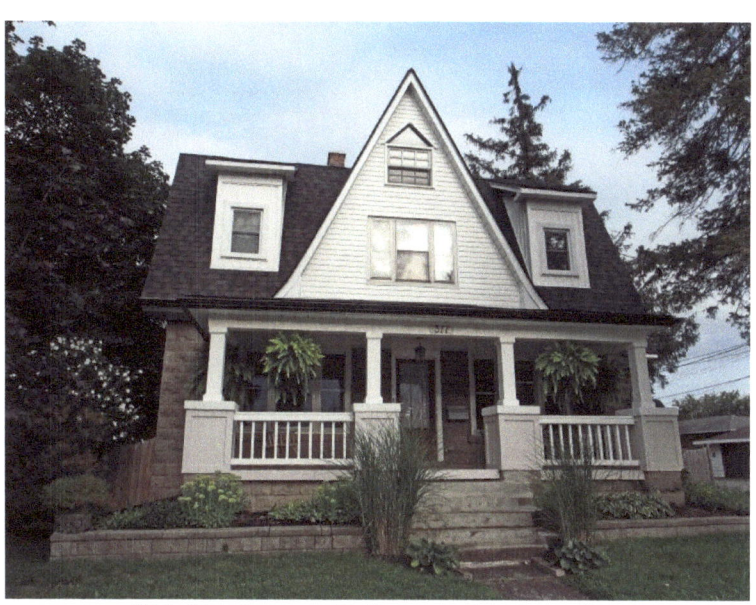

311 Canborough Street - Vernacular

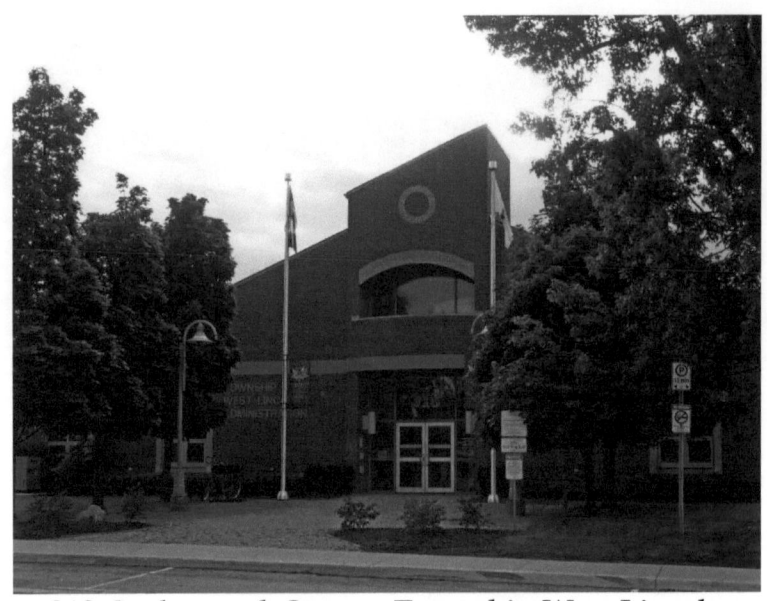
318 Canborough Street – Township West Lincoln Administration

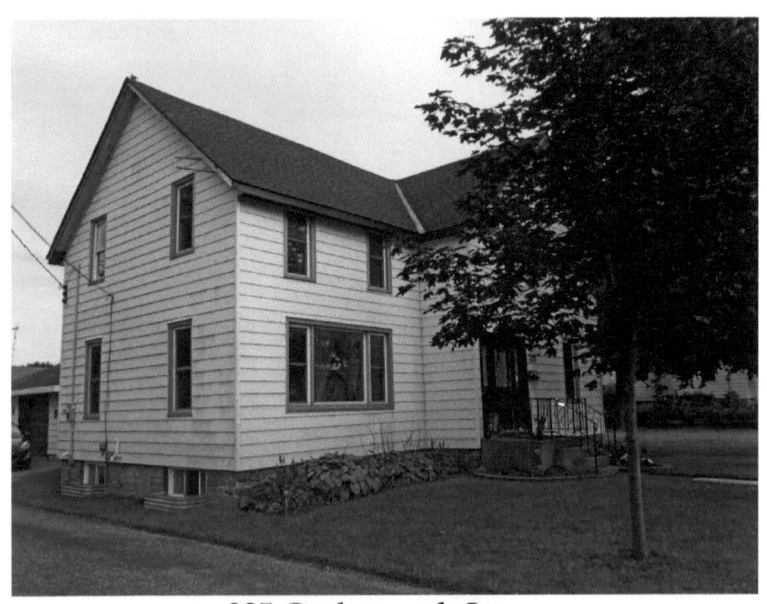
325 Canborough Street

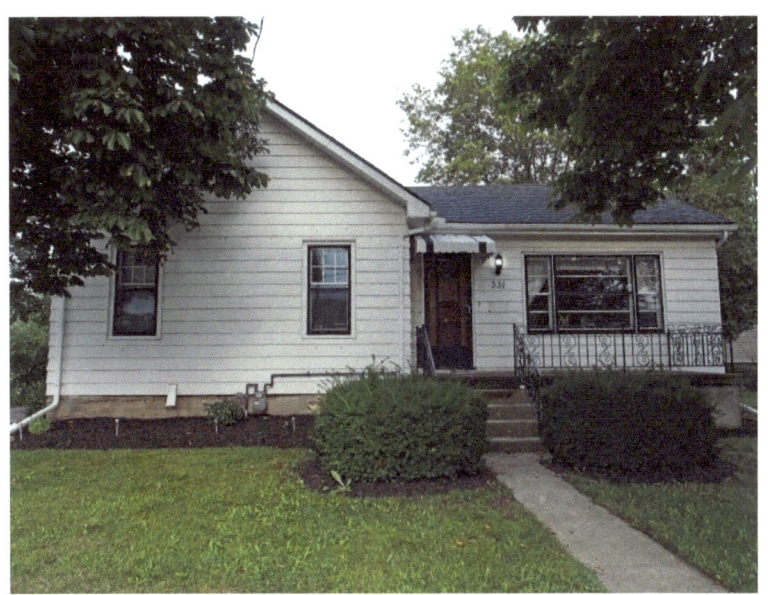

331 Canborough Street

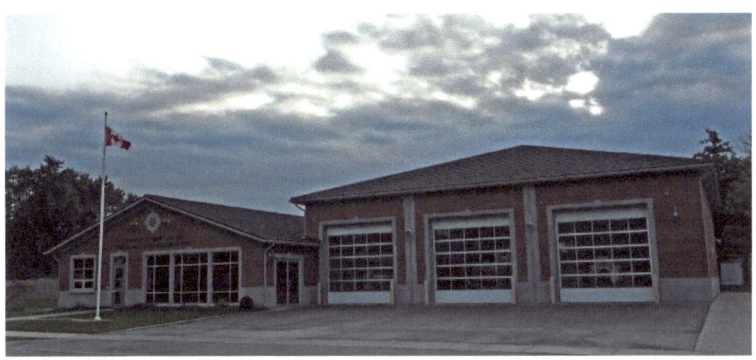

Canborough Street – Township of West Lincoln Fire Department Headquarters

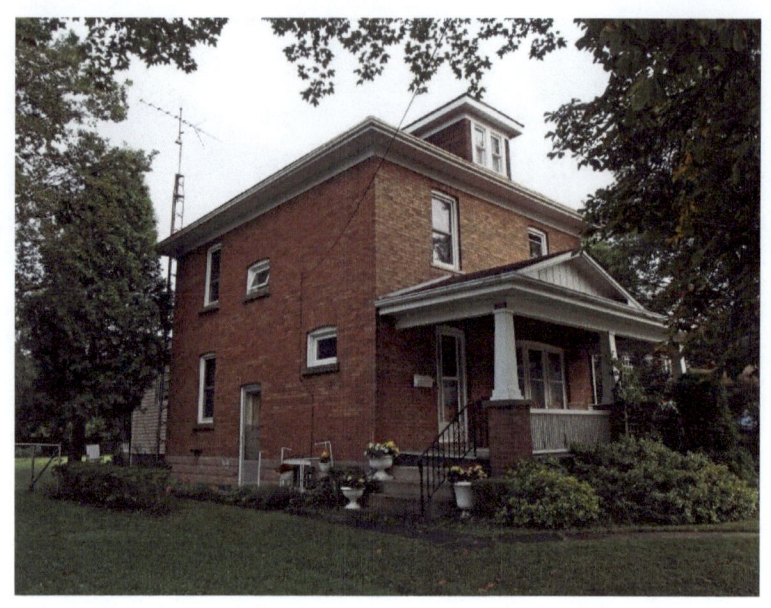

Canborough Street – dormer, pediment

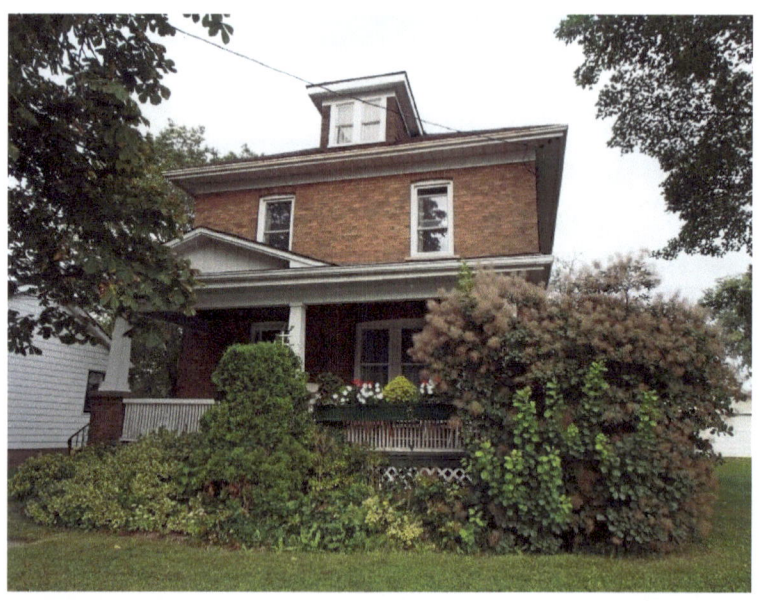

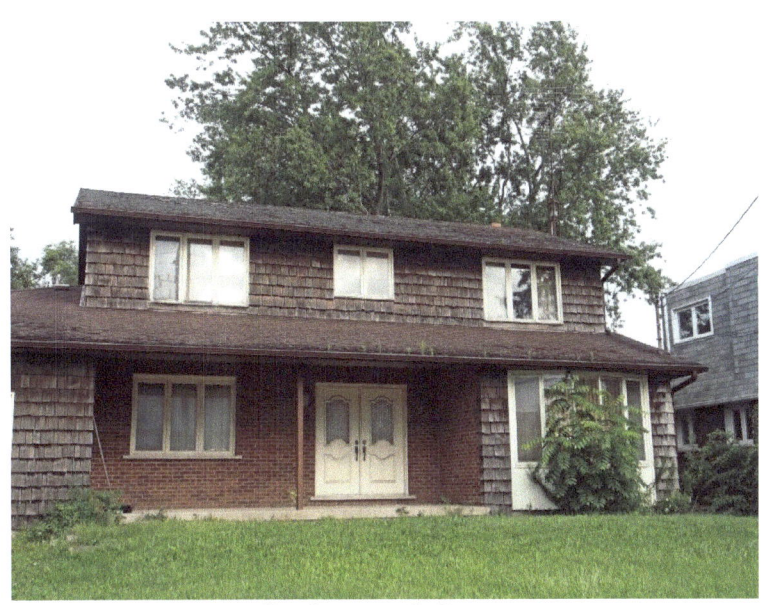

Canborough Street

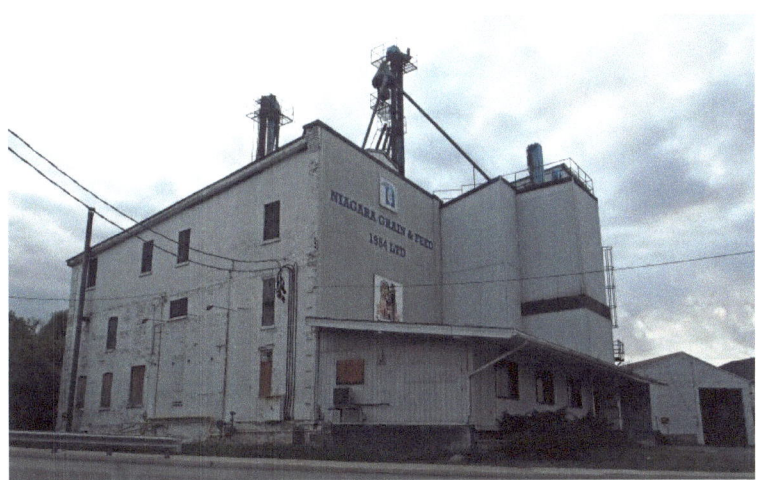

Mill

Architectural Terms

Bay Window: A window that projects out from a wall, in a semicircular, rectangular, or polygonal design. Used frequently in Gothic and Victorian designs. Example: 233 Station Street, Page 11	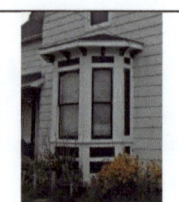
Belvedere: (from the Italian "beautiful view") an architectural feature on a roof, in a garden or on a terrace that gives a beautiful view. Example: 255 Canborough Street, Page 46	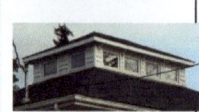
Brackets: a decorative or weight-bearing structural element which forms a right angle with one side against a wall and the other under a projecting surface such as an eave or roof. Example: 161 Griffin Street, Page 23	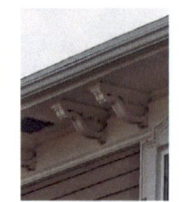
Buttress: a masonry structure built against or projecting from a wall which serves to support or reinforce the wall. In Canadian architecture, they are sometimes used for decoration. Example: 116 West Street, Page 15	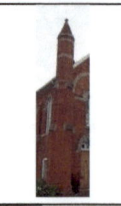
Capital: The uppermost finish or decoration on a column. An Ionic column has a small base, a thin elegant shaft, and a capital composed of volutes which are carved whirls or twists that take the form of a scroll. Example: 235 Canborough Street, Page 46 A Doric column is characterized by a plain column with no base, a shaft with twenty flutings, and a simple capital with a simple entablature. Example: 279 Station Street, Page 7	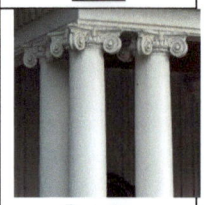 Ionic 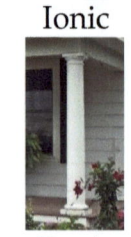 Doric

Cornice Return: decorative element on the end of a gable. Example: 205 Canborough Street, Page 43	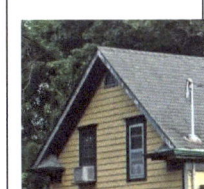
Cupola: A domed or curved roof rising from a building as a decorative element. Example: 235 Canborough Street, Page 46	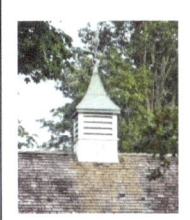
Dichromatic brickwork: the use of two colours of brick, tile or slate to decorate a façade. Example: 116 West Street, Page 15	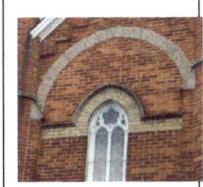
Dormer: (French for "sleep") a gable end window that pierces through the plane of a sloping roof surface to create usable space in the top floor or attic of a building by adding headroom. Example: 251 Station Street, Page 9	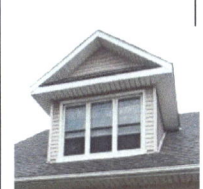
Gable: the triangular portion of a wall between the edges of a sloping roof. Example: Station Street, Page 8	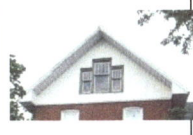

Gambrel Roof: a symmetrical two-sided roof with two slopes on each side; the upper slope is positioned at a shallow angle, while the lower slope is steep. It is similar to a mansard roof, but a gambrel has vertical gable ends instead of being hipped at the four corners of the building. Example: St. Catharine Street, Page 29	
Hipped Roof: a roof where all sides slope downwards to the walls with no gables. Example: 279 Station Street, Page 7	
Keystones and Voussoirs: a voussoir is a wedge-shaped element used in building an arch. A keystone is the central stone that locks all the stones into position, allowing the arch to bear weight. A keystone is often enlarged and embellished. Example: 104 Griffin Street, Page 28	
Lancet Window: a tall, narrow window with a pointed arch at its top. Example: 246 Station Street, Page 10	

Mansard Roof: This style was popularized by Francois Mansart (1598-1666), an accomplished architect of the French Baroque period and especially fashionable during the Second French Empire (1852-1870). This roof is almost flat on the top section, with two slopes on each of its sides with the lower slope at a steeper angle than the upper, and has dormer windows. Example: 401 Canborough Street, Page 42	
Muntin: When a window unit has more than one pane, the material that separates the panes is called the muntin. The larger, more decorative separations are called mullions. In stained glass windows, each piece of colored glass is held in place by a muntin. These were traditionally made of iron. Example: 116 West Street, Page 15	
Palladian Window: a large window that is divided into three sections with the centre section larger than the two side sections and usually arched. Example: 121 West Street, Page 16	
Pediment: a triangular section above the door or portico, usually supported by columns. The inside of the triangle is called the tympanum. Example: 287 Station Street, Page 7	
Rose Window: a circular window with ornamental tracery radiating from the centre. Example: 143 St. Catharine Street, Page 32	

Sidelight: a vertical window that flanks a door, and is often used to emphasize the importance of a primary entrance. **Transom Window:** the light above the doorway, also called a fanlight. Example: 143 St. Catharine Street, Page 32	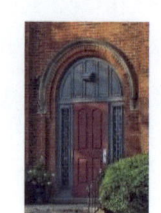
Turret: a small tower that projects from the wall of a building. Example: 228 Station Street, Page 6	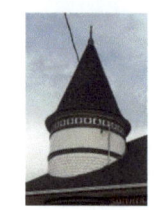
Verge board and Finial: also called bargeboards – hang from the projecting end of a roof and are often elaborately carved and ornamented. **Finial:** ornament added to the top of a gable, pinnacle, canopy or spire – a Gothic element. Example: 235 Canborough Street, Page 46	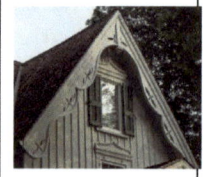

Building Styles

Arts and Crafts: The overlying theme - the house was based on the function of the house. Rooms were oriented to take advantage of the movement of the sun for warmth and light during daylight hours. Side entrances allowed for useable space on the front facade for light or garden use. Arts and Crafts houses have many of these features: wood, stone or stucco siding; low-pitched roof; wide eaves with triangular brackets; exposed roof rafters; porch with thick square or round columns; stone porch supports; exterior chimney made with stone; open floor plans with few hallways; many windows, some with stained or leaded glass; beamed ceilings; dark wood wainscoting and moldings; built-in cabinets, shelves, and seating. Example: 120 St. Catharine Street, Page 30	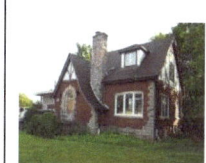
Edwardian, 1900-1930 – This style bridges the ornate and elaborate styles of the Victorian era and the simplified styles of the 20th century. Edwardian Classicism provided simple, balanced facades, simple rooflines, dormer windows, large front porches, and smooth brick surfaces. Voussoirs and keystones are used sparingly and are understated. Finials and cresting are absent. Cornice brackets and braces are block-like and openings have flat arches or plain stone lintels. Example: 121 West Street, Page 16	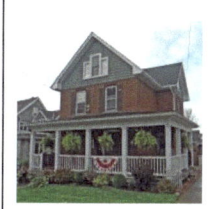

Gothic Revival, 1830-1890 – These decorative buildings have sharply-pitched gables with highly detailed verge boards, pointed-arch window openings, and dichromatic brickwork. It is a common style in Ontario. Example: 139 St. Catharine Street, Page 31	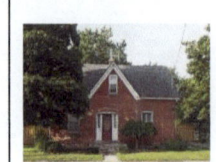
Neo-colonial (also Colonial Revival, Georgian Revival or Neo-Georgian) architecture seeks to revive elements of architectural style of American colonial architecture of the period around the Revolutionary War which drew strongly from Georgian architecture of Great Britain. Architecture from the 18th and early 19th centuries in Ontario includes a wide assortment of detailing and ornament applied to a design centered around the fireplace and the source of water. Structures are typically two stories, have a symmetrical front facade with elaborate front doorways, often with decorative crown pediments, fanlights, and sidelights, symmetrical windows flanking the front entrance, often in pairs or threes, and columned porches. Example: St. Catharine Street, Page 29	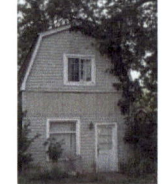
Regency Cottage, 1830-1860 – This style originated in England in 1815 and spread to Ontario later in the 19th century as British officers retired to Canada. It is a modest one-storey house with a low-pitched hip roof and has a symmetrical front façade. Example: 151 West Street, Page 17	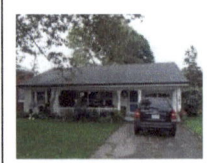

Romanesque Revival, 1880-1910 – This style hearkens back to medieval architecture of the 11th and 12th centuries with a heavy appearance, blocky towers and rounded arches. Example: 143 St. Catharine Street, Page 32	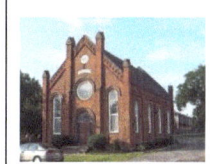
Tudor Revival – exposed timbers with stucco infill, multi-paned windows. Example: 135 West Street, Page 16	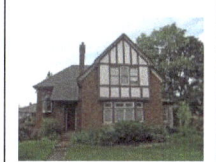
Vernacular/Traditional Mode 1638 - 1950 Influenced but not defined by a particular style, vernacular buildings are made from easily available materials and exhibit local design characteristics. Example: 311 Canborough Street, Page 47	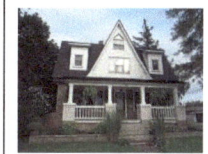

www.ingramcontent.com/pod-product-compliance
Lightning Source LLC
Chambersburg PA
CBHW041942240526
45473CB00033B/307